30

If I Had Only One Sermon

to Preach On Immortality

IF I HAD ONLY ONE
SERMON TO PREACH
ON IMMORTALITY

Edited, with an Introduction, by

William L. Stidger

New York and London
Harper & Brothers Publishers
1929

DEDICATED TO

DR. ALBERT C. KNUDSON

DEAN OF BOSTON UNIVERSITY
SCHOOL OF THEOLOGY

TEACHER, PREACHER, PHILOSOPHER, FRIEND

INTRODUCTION

"Immortality" is one of the fascinating words of the English language.

"Immortality" is more than a word. It is an idea, a dream, a hope, an expectation, a faith which has intrigued the heart of humanity from the beginning of time.

"Immortality" has been expressed by poet, preacher, and prophet. It has been the central theme and dream of fiction and philosophy and drama. No history of humanity could be written without this hope running through it like a silver thread through a beautiful fabric.

Neither a final definition of the word, nor the final scope of the idea of Immortality, may be revealed to man; yet the human mind never tires of penetrating this mystery. The idea of Eternal Life has rooted itself deep in the soil of humanity.

"What would you preach if you had only one sermon to preach on Immortality?" was asked of 22 leading ministers. Each answered by submitting a sermon containing his best thought and conviction, not a passing definition, but a carefully presented *argumentum ad rem*.

In choosing the contributors to the volume of sermons, certain groupings were kept in mind, in order that a wider representation of preachers—geographically, theologically, denominationally, and by age groups—would be made possible.

That the messages of leading English preachers should be heard was obvious. Those of this group who responded to an invitation to submit a sermon were Dr. John Hutton, editor of the *British Weekly*, Dr. F. W. Norwood, pastor of the City Temple, London, Dr. Leyton Richards, pastor of Carr's Lane, Birmingham, England. In order that Canada might be represented in this selection, Dr. Lynn Harold Hough, pastor of the American Presbyterian Church of Montreal, was asked to contribute.

It also seemed wise to have at least one sermon by a layman and one by a woman. Mr. George W. Coleman, head of the Ford Hall Forum, Boston, and Miss Maude Royden were named to represent each of these groups. In order to know the thinking of the younger ministers of America, men who are to be the leaders of tomorrow, the following were invited into the group: Dr. Henry Hitt Crane, pastor of the Elm Park Methodist Episcopal Church, Scranton, Pennsylvania; Dr. Elwood Rowsey, pastor of the First Westminster Presbyterian Church, Toledo, Ohio; Dr. Daniel Poling, preacher at the Marble Collegiate Church, New York City.

It is a privilege to have the Catholic Church represented by one of its highest officials in the United States, His Eminence, William Cardinal O'Connell, of

Boston, and the Hebrew Churches by Rabbi Harry
Levi, of Boston. In so far as possible, representatives
of leading denominations and types of theological belief throughout the country are to be found within the
covers of this book. Among them are the immortals
of the Protestant ministry, names of men always to
be found in any selected list of America's great
preachers, names that could not possibly be omitted
from a volume of this type without the volume losing
caste.

It has been a pleasure to edit this book. I am grate-
ful to Mr. Wm. C. Hanson for suggesting the idea of
a unified theme. The men who have contributed have
done so with unfailing courtesy and promptness. Most
of them have taken the general theme: "If I Had
Only One Sermon to Preach on Immortality" seriously. The total result is strangely varied in its approach. When a unified theme was first proposed it
was thought that there would be much duplication of
subject matter and treatment. That fear has not been
realized. On the contrary, there is as wide a variety
of approach to this universally interesting theme as
there are differences in the personalities of the contributors, in spite of the fact that several have taken
the same text.

After one has read these sermons and come forth
from the cathedral of the book, it is as though he had
worshiped in the little chapels of a great cathedral.
He has looked upon beautiful windows, has heard
great organ music rolling through ancient corridors,

and has heard great voices resonant with truth. He comes forth with a new certainty of life's eternal values and a new faith in the immortality of the soul.

W. L. S.

CONTENTS

xi

CONTENTS

xii

"If a Man Die Shall He Live Again?"

WILLIAM EDWARD BIEDER-WOLF, D.D.

William Edward Biederwolf was born at Monticello, Ind., September 29th, 1867. He graduated from Princeton University in 1892 with an A.M. and received his Theological Degree from Princeton Theological Seminary three years later. He studied later in Berlin University. He was ordained to the Presbyterian ministry in 1897 and was a pastor for ten or fifteen years after which he went into Evangelistic work.

In the field of Evangelism he has become as widely known to this generation as any preacher save only "Billy" Sunday himself; and in addition to this he has for years been the President of the Family Altar League of America. He has been President of Winona College, Dean of the Winona School of Theology and of the famous Winona Lake Bible Conferences for many years.

He has written many books, most of them sermons on Evangelistic themes, illustrations, and Family Altar League books.

He is often compared with "Billy" Sunday in the Evangelistic field, and

is in many ways like Sunday except
that he perhaps has a more balanced
intellectual background than Sunday,
in addition to the same religious fer-
vor and passion for men.

"If a Man Die Shall He Live Again?"

—JOB XIV: 14

By W. E. BIEDERWOLF, PRESIDENT, LAKE WINONA BIBLE
CONFERENCE AND SCHOOL OF THEOLOGY

IN THIS text is found the all-absorbing question of
the ages. Every arch built up in religion's name
has had immortality for its keystone.

Buddhists, Mohammedans, Christians; Theoso-
phists, Agnostics, Infidels; men of every faith and men
who say they have no faith at all will sit around the
table and discuss for hours the question, "Are the Dead
Alive?" "Do We Survive the Chemical Change
Called Death?"

It makes all the difference of both worlds to me
whether my life is ephemeral, a candle suddenly
snuffed out, a gleam of consciousness between the
cradle and the grave, or whether in me there is something that is going to survive the limitations of time
and space and the corruption of matter; whether *this*
life is the palace of existence, or whether, as Browning
says in his "Christmas Eve and Easter Day," it is but
the vestibule of the palace.

Does man, as Shelley says, "lie down on the lone
couch of his everlasting sleep"?

3

IF I HAD ONLY ONE SERMON TO PREACH

Is it true, as Moschus puts it in his mournful "Elegy on Man,"

> Man wakes no more! Man,
>   Valiant, glorious, wise;
> When death once chills him, sinks in sleep profound—
>   A long, unconscious, never-ending sleep.

Shall we write over our cemeteries as they did in Paris in the days of the Revolution, "Death Is an Eternal Sleep," or shall we, with our own poet believe,

> There is no death; what seems so is transition,

and have something of Lord Tennyson's sublime faith, when in his matchless poem, "In Memoriam," mourning for his young friend, Arthur Hallam, he says:

> That each who seems a separate whole,
>   Should move his rounds and fusing all
> The skirts of self again, should fall,
>   Remerging in the general soul!
> Is faith as vague as all unsweet.

Ah, no, he says,

> Eternal form shall still divide
>   The Eternal soul from all beside,
> And I shall know him when we meet.

There is a profound silence about the grave. Does it not sometimes seem that we "cry aloud and the only answer is the echo of our wailing cry?" The strongholds of princes and the rock-hewn Morros tumble down like houses made of cards before the powerful guns of modern science, but just back of the grave is a granite wall before which nature and science all stand dumb.

How strange that Lazarus brought no message back. His silence is significant, but a curiosity like ours, children as we are, still "crying in the night" can well be excused.

> Of all who have crossed the river,
>   And learn the eternal lore,
> Not one has returned to tell us
>   Of the land on the other shore.
> Not a single hand has lifted
>   The curtain that hangs between,
> Not a voice revealed the wonders
>   That no human eye hath seen.

Oh, the deep silence of the infinite beyond!

> We have prayed and watched and waited,
>   And called to heaven their name;
> And stilled our pulse to listen,
>   But never an answer came.

But silence, you know, sometimes speaks louder than thunder. Little Roland climbed upon the knee of Charlemagne and asked him concerning the kingdom which would be his when he was big like his father, but the great king was silent and thoughtful. How could the little fellow understand or half conceive the future glory to which he was to fall heir! But in the moment of Charlemagne's thoughtful silence and concealment were revelations of grandeur and magnificence words could have but feebly expressed had a maturer mind than the child-king's been there to grasp

5

them. Eternity is a profound subject; too profound for man's profoundest mind. And its silence is big with meaning. In answering the question of our text we shall not deal with science; not because its testimony is unfavorable, for if science once doubted, it is now beginning to mount up on wings of faith, until we hear John Fiske, the master scientist, declaring that, "The materialistic assumption that the life of the soul is perhaps the most colossal instance of baseless assumption in all the history of scientific thought."

Neither shall the arguments of philosophy be marshalled, though the testimony of the world's recognized noblest philosophy has always been an inspiration to the belief in the soul's immortality. Even the philosophy that once shrouded the tomb with midnight darkness has itself become a star of hope, and the skull and crossbones have given place to the white lily and the red rose.

There are three great arguments favoring immortality, and one great testimony which settles the matter for the man of faith. A few moments first with these arguments.

If you have ever climbed the winding stairs of Washington's Monument you will recall the little windows cut through its granite sides, through which streams the light of the outer world to illumine the dark interior, and through which the eye now and then catches a glimpse of a great city, of a river winding like a silver ribbon through the fields, forests and plains stretching out beyond the range of vision with all their beauty and abounding life.

And so to the soul groping on "the altar stairs that slope through darkness up to God," there comes betime the streaming lines of light that speak of a world brighter and more glorious than its own. Each source of truth is a little window of immortality opened up in the soul's darkened chamber through which it catches glimpses of a vast, illimitable life beyond.

Through three of these windows let us now look and see if man is not immortal.

1. Man's Instinct of Immortality. Man has an inborn sense of a higher destiny. If tired of other arguments he needs only turn back to commune with his own soul's consciousness, and deep within himself he hears a voice, as unmistakable though as gentle as an evening's zephyr, which is like that of the sentinel in Tennyson's immortal poem—

> Who moves about from place to place,
> And whispers to the worlds of space,
> In the deep night, that all is well.

Have you ever seen the robin flying away before the chilling blasts of winter? Did you ever see the bee sailing out into the vast sea of air, going from flower to flower, and then by its own peculiar instinct find its way straight back to its home? Never has bird or beast or insect been deceived or led astray by their God-given instinct, and do you think that God would plant that holiest of instincts in the human soul and then permit it to mislead that soul in its

7

longing and aspiration after immortality and the life beyond?

It was Horace Bushnell who said, "The faith of immortality depends upon a sense of it begotten and not on an argument for it concluded."

It was this "sense of it" that held the mind of Wordsworth when he wrote, "By trailing clouds of glory do we come from God who is our home."

And this was the thought of Browning when he said, "I see my way as birds their trackless way," and beholding the wild fowl winging its trackless way through space, Bryant, our own poet of nature, breathed out these lines:

> He who from zone to zone,
>   Guides through the boundless sky
> Thy certain flight;
>   In the long way that I must tread alone,
> Will lead my steps aright.

Of course He will. I know that I am deathless because I feel it in my soul, and what my soul feels I will believe.

Do you know how astronomers discovered Neptune? They noticed the strange perturbations of Uranus and concluded that it must be influenced by another planet, and so closely did La Verier calculate the place of that planet in the distant heavens that when Dr. Galle, of Berlin, pointed his telescope to the designated place he found Neptune shining through the lens. In some such way immortality and

8

heaven were discovered. What a powerful influence eternal life by its attractions exerts upon the human soul! and though much is still mysterious, of this much, that it *must* exist, the soul is certain, because to its best thought and highest ambition the unseen world responds, and we believe it with a conviction that cannot be shaken.

2. Man's Longing for Immortality. The world has always believed in immortality because it has always longed to be immortal.

In the pyramids of Egypt three thousand years before Christ was born are hoary inscriptions relative to the dim unknown and addresses to the boatman Charon, who ferries the dead across the stream into the happy fields of Yaru. The idea is traceable through Homer, Hesiod, and Pindar.

Plato makes three strong arguments for the soul's immortality the raft on which he sails through life. We are told that Cleombrotus, a heathen thinker, after reading these arguments of Plato, ran and cast himself down from a high rock that he might die and enter upon that immortality which he loved and believed would follow after death.

All down the ages has come the voice of humanity's heart crying for life beyond the grave, and if the immortality of the soul is but the speculation of human genius how are you going to account for this longing in the breast of every savage people who ever lived upon this earth?

9

They that in barbarian burials killed the slave and slew the
    wife,
Felt within themselves the sacred passion of the second life.

Whence comes this longing so universal and so persistent, if not from God? Nature works on hinges.
Its every longing has its natural satisfaction. Its arrangement for supply and demand is marvelous indeed. There is liquid for thirst and food for hunger,
and shall God fill the soul with a hunger and a thirst
which either His indifference or His powerlessness
leads Him to disappoint? No, indeed! And if Plato
could be outreasoned, the unanswerable of all philosophy be disproven, and the Revelation of God be destroyed, man's longing for immortality would still be
one of immortality's strongest proofs.

3. Man's Need of Immortality. This idea is big
with meaning. The best development this life affords
to man is but fragmentary, and the reasonable inference is another life to complete it.

It is so with the intellect. The mind of man possesses faculties demanding eternal time for development. They are God-given and God will satisfy them
with more than a little handful of earthly time.

How pathetic the early death of those whom Tennyson has called "the forbidden builders." I mean
the ten-talented men whose early achievements were
so rich with promise for the future. What promise for
literature there was in young Arthur Hallam! Frederick W. Robertson, the scholar-preacher, must die at
thirty-seven; Raphael, at the same age, and Mozart

when but thirty-six, while Keats finished his earthly career of such great promise at the early age of twenty-two.

Out in your garden is a tree bringing forth its fruit in its season. It has all the time it needs for development. If it lived a million years it could only leaf, blossom, bud, and bear fruit. Will God give to a tree time for perfect growth, and to the man who planted the tree deny the time for the utmost perfection of the life within his soul?

Raphael's vision of the Madonna never touched the canvas, and the polished symphonies of Beethoven are not to be compared, he himself tells us, with the heavenly music which swept through his soul.

In fact in everyone lies a germ of wondrous possibility needing only higher conditions for development, and the mightiest intellects here are but feeble indications of what you and I may become when such conditions are realized. Rather than ask for the "glory of warrior, the glory of orator, the glory of song," who would not, like her of whom the poet sings, crave "the glory of going on and still to be"?

If death ends all, then for some suicide would be the greatest blessing; for the world is teeming with millions to whom society has denied the opportunity even for development here. Women, like the one of whom Thomas Hood sings in his "Song of the Shirt,"

In poverty, hunger and dirt; sewing a shroud as well as a shirt.

11

Children of whom Oliver Twist, living in Fagin's den with thieves for associates, is a type.

Furthermore humanity needs another world for the administration of justice. If there is no life beyond the grave what recompense had Paul for the stones and stripes that stung him well-nigh to death, or Savonarola for the flames that licked up his blood on the Square of San Marco by the palace and the church?

Immortality has at least one vigorous root in man's imperious need to believe in a more ideal justice than earth has ever yet afforded. What do we see? Tyrants enthroned and saints sent to the dungeon; vice wearing the purple and virtue clothed in rags; Socrates drinking the hemlock and his persecutors enjoying the palace. Cicero with his head chopped off; Dante driven from his land by wicked princes; Shakespeare, that consummate flower of his age, unappreciated, scorned and starved; Columbus, bound in chains, heartbroken at the ingratitude of his fellows; Nero, Borgia, and the Pope sitting upon thrones; Paul beheaded and Huss burned at the stake!

Pathetic, indeed, are such unjust inequalities. Much more so if there is no other world to right the wrongs of this. If man longs for immortality, how much more does he need it! Friendship, love, grace, intellect, every faculty and every virtue are all alike imperfect here. The soul needs immortality and immortality alone can finish out what life has left unfinished here.

Man's heaven-born instinct! Man's impassionate longing! Man's imperious need! Are these not enough to make one reasonably sure of the infinite beyond? And we answer, Yes, if back of the universe and back of life there is an intelligent and just and reasonable God. If this last be true, the first must be so. And such a God is the God we know.

Listen once more to Tennyson:

> Thou wilt not leave us in the dust;
> Thou madest man, he knows not why,
> He thinks he was not made to die,
> And Thou hast made him; Thou art just.

God's order of things is rational. That was a great testimony of philosopher and scientist, John Fiske, when he said, "For my part, therefore, I believe in the immortality of the soul, not in the sense in which I accept the demonstrable truths of science, but as a supreme act of faith in the reasonableness of God's work." Has all this work been for nothing, he asks.

Is it reasonable that the tree shall outlive the man who planted it, the garment outlast the man who wears it? Is it reasonable that Tennyson's *In Memoriam* should be immortal and immortality be denied to its author? Shall the *Origin of Species* endure and Darwin die? Is the *Principia* greater than Newton? Is it reasonable that man should die for the truth in this world and not behold the truth enthroned in another world to come? Is it reasonable that the lone mound in the jungles of Africa or the unknown grave in the Indian Ocean should be the end of Livingstone

13

dying alone upon his knees, or of lion-hearted Judson giving his last drop of blood for dying India's sake? Is it reasonable that Savonarola and Huss and Wyclif and all "the slaughtered saints whose bones lie scattered on the Alpine mountains cold" should die the martyr's death and not receive the martyr's crown? Is it reasonable that Nero and Diocletian, who threw the Christians to the lions, should wade in innocent blood and not suffer for their crimes? Shall the Son of God be crucified and not be exalted?

No, indeed, if there is any reason for existence at all, there is reason for going on. It is not so strange that man should continue to be as it is that he ever began to be, and if there is any reason in the universe, if there is any reason in God, there is reason for man to go on.

> Who made life, plain, and made the sea
> Denied not man a destiny
> To match his thought. Though mists obscure
> And storms retard, the event is sure.
> Each surging wave cries evermore,
> "Death also has its further shore."

The one great testimony which settles the matter for the man of faith is the Word of God, the Bible. It was Joseph Cook who said, "Pillow my head on no guess when I die." Well, the Word of God leaves us in no uncertainty as to the reality of the soul's future existence.

In the parable of the rich man and Lazarus it is

made quite clear that memory and reason are operative in the world to come.

Again, it is said in the Word that "It is appointed unto men once to die," but it does not stop with this; it says, "and after this the judgment." What use of a judgment if there are no souls in existence after death to be judged?

Listen to Paul, "Now this I say, brethren, that flesh and blood cannot inherit the kingdom of God; neither doth corruption inherit incorruption. . . . For this corruptible must put on incorruption, and this mortal must put on immortality. So when this corruptible shall have put on incorruption, and this mortal shall have put on immortality, then shall be brought to pass the saying that is written, Death is swallowed up in victory. O death, where is thy sting? O grave, where is thy victory?"

Of Jesus it is said that by his death and resurrection he "abolished death and brought life and immortality to light," and it was this same Jesus who said, "In my Father's house are many mansions: if it were not so, I would have told you. I go to prepare a place for you."

Did Jesus have divine authority thus to speak? This indisputable prerogative we cannot argue here. With equal right he revealed unto us the character of a God, who, if He is the God Jesus declared Him to be, will not permit us to perish when we are laid in the grave.

"Behold what manner of love the Father hath bestowed upon us that we should be called the sons of God. . . . Beloved, now we are the sons of God, and it doth not yet appear what we shall be; but we know that, when he shall appear, we shall be like him; for we shall see him as he is."

But to continue after death does not necessarily mean to have immortality. To be etymologically and Scripturally accurate immortality must be applied only to the body. "Mortality" comes from the Latin word, "mors," meaning bodily death, or a dead body. "Immortality" means just the reverse, "not subject to decay." This immortality of the body comes with the resurrection. Thus Paul, speaking of the saints' resurrection, says, "When this corruptible shall have put on incorruption, and this mortal shall have put on immortality," the parallel expressions being synonymous. Thus when the mortal, that which is subject to decay, dies, it is resurrected and made immortal because of and through the soul's faith in Jesus Christ, who, we are told in I Timothy 6: 16, alone hath immortality.

But what of the soul? It, too, dies. It died in Adam. But that does not mean that it ceased to exist. Spiritual death is not annihilation. It means to be cut off from the favor and the fellowship of God.

The soul receives its resurrection at the moment of its regeneration through faith in Jesus Christ. Not to believe in Jesus Christ does not mean to pass out of existence. To exist, therefore, does not necessarily

16

mean to have life. Dead things exist. The Sphinx out on the Egyptian desert has been in existence for unnumbered centuries and will no doubt be in existence when the last trump is sounded and the silent sepulchers by its side give up their dead, but it has no life and never will have.

True it is that the soul of the wicked will forever have conscious existence, but this is not the life that is found in Christ. The difference is just this—and it is a difference that is as high as heaven and as deep as hell—you will find it stated in I John 5:11, 12, "And this is the record, that God hath given to us eternal life, and this life is in his Son. He that hath the Son hath life; and he that hath not the Son hath not life, but the wrath of God *abideth on him*."

Reader, do you want this eternal life? Then let the Son Himself tell you how to get it, "And this is life eternal that they may know Thee, the only true God, and Jesus Christ whom Thou hast sent" (John 17:3).

In the old days of heartless tyranny it seemed as though the princes and kings vied with each other to see who could resort to the most terrible and cruel methods of torture. One of the methods of punishment with the Hohenstaufen house in Germany was to put their victim into a nicely furnished and comfortable room. The prisoner might think this a punishment not to be despised, but the vindictive persecutors knew better and in a few days the victim realized as much, for he noticed by and by that the room had contracted, that the walls were coming nearer together and his horrible fate all at once flashed upon his mind. In oiled and silent grooves the metal walls were drawing closer and closer. At last he could no longer lie down; the next day he had room only to stand erect. Frantic, he put his hands against the iron walls to hold them, but silently, remorselessly they closed upon him and crushed him to death.

What a picture this of the world and the man in it who has no hope in Christ—no hope for the world to come. The years such a man lives are the walls of his prison and every day they are contracting about him.

Things may seem pleasant for a time but with every pulse beat the iron walls draw closer and closer about his soul. Every hour gone is one chance less to win eternal life—to win glory and honor and immortality. The only hope of escape is through Jesus Christ, and every voice of mercy, every striving of the spirit, is an angel of God knocking at the door of your narrowing prison to tell you of the refuge that you can find in Jesus Christ.

As you finish with the reading of this sermon you can take Christ to be your Saviour; by faith you can accept him as your Redeemer, your Lord and your Master, and that

Will be the hour
When the tree of life will burst into flower,
And rain at your feet a glorious dower
Of something grander than ever you knew.

The Certitude of Immortality

S. PARKES CADMAN, D.D., Litt.D., LL.D.

S. Parkes Cadman was born in
Shropshire, England, December 18th,
1884, graduated from Richmond
College of London University and
migrated to the United States of
America where he has been one of
our most distinguished clergymen for
many years.

He first attracted wide attention
by his Sunday afternoon open
forums at the Bedford Street Branch
of the Y. M. C. A. especially when
these addresses and forums were
broadcast by the radio. In the years
since the radio has come into general use Dr. Cadman has become,
without doubt, the foremost Radio
Preacher of America, reaching audiences estimated in terms of millions
of people.

He served as Chaplain of the 23rd
Regiment of New York City during
the war and won the love and ad-
miration of great hosts of boys and
their friends during this time. He
served for many years as the President of the Federal Council of
Churches of Christ in America until
recently succeeded by Bishop Francis
J. McConnell.

He is the author of *Charles Dar-*

*win and Other English Thinkers,
The Victory of Christmas, Ambassa-
dors of God, Christianity and the
State, Imagination and Religion,* and
The Christ of God.

Dr. Cadman is so well grounded
in his intellectual life, and yet knows
the vocabulary and the world of the
common man of America so thoroughly that he is equally at home
in an academic atmosphere or in a
street meeting. He is more famed
for his "Question and Answer
Forum" over the radio than for any
other single thing of his ministry.
No book would be complete without
a sermon in it by this giant of the
churches.

The Certitude of Immortality

By S. Parkes Cadman, Radio Preacher, Federal
Council of Churches in America

"If a man die, shall he live again?"
—Job XIV: 14

AN AFFIRMATIVE answer to this question was once
comparatively easy. Belief in immortality was
then practically universal in Christendom.

Controversy raged around other New Testament
teachings. Christ's solemn declaration, however, that
"God is not the God of the dead, but of the living,"
was everywhere accepted by his disciples with unspeakable relief and thanksgiving. The historic con-
fession, "I believe in the life everlasting," expressed
the gist of that declaration in one of the earliest creeds
of the Church. Throughout succeeding centuries it
has been repeated with no trace of reluctance or uncertainty. Schools of philosophy, art, music, and common tradition were founded upon this assurance of immortality. All ranks and conditions of society
regarded the issue as settled. No misgivings plagued
the confidence of learned or simple. Into the bound-
less future thus conceived theologians and poets,
painters and composers, projected their visions of para-

21

dise, purgatory and perdition. Pastors and evangelists used to good effect the doctrine established by the word of our Lord himself.

Other characteristic beliefs fostered the fixed faith in immortality. This planet was viewed as specially created for human habitation. Its time processes and also those of the universe were severely limited. Its ageless wonders of development were crowded into a few millenniums. These arbitrary reckonings embarrassed the general idea of the scheme of things. The relief of the situation lay in its impermanence. A sudden and unexpected cataclysm would presently end its confusion. None knew what a day or an hour might bring forth. Christian thinkers declared that the real reason for humanity's existence is not discernible in the visible world. The faithful were likened to strangers and pilgrims who had no continuing city here. The soul was a spark of heavenly flame, eager for release from its mortal frame, ever longing for the city which hath foundations, whose builder and maker is God. In such spiritual sceneries as these, filled with glory and with terror, belief in the survival of human personality beyond physical dissolution flourished, and gave tremendous significance to the rewards and penalties of an endless future. The possibility that unbroken spiritual existence, and whatever it implied, was but the creation of imagination, actuated by man's instinct for immortality, was not seriously considered save by a skeptical minority.

II

Our generation confronts a radically different outlook on eternity. Human life is no longer regarded by certain materialistic thinkers as creation's culmination. For them it is no more than a minor phase in the slowly unfolding drama of cosmic life and being. One wonders if Macaulay could have felt in our time the freedom which was his, when he paid his famous tribute to the Puritans:

If their names were not found in the registers of heralds they were recorded in the Book of Life. If their steps were not attended by a splendid train of menials, legions of ministering angels had charge over them. Their palaces were houses not made with hands; their diadems, crowns of glory which should never fade away. On the rich and the eloquent, on nobles and priests, they looked down with contempt, for they esteemed themselves rich in a more precious treasure, and eloquent in a more sublime language; nobles by the right of an earlier creation, and priests by the imposition of a mightier hand. The very meanest of them was a being to whose fate a mysterious and terrible importance belonged, on whose slightest actions the spirits of light and darkness gazed with anxious interest, who had been destined, before heaven and earth were created, to enjoy a felicity which should continue when heaven and earth should have passed away.

Here in unmistakable terms we are recalled to the Faith which vanquished formidable antagonists and transferred authority in every realm to new centers. Yet its expression by Macaulay's brilliant pen provokes in many modern minds an amazed incredulity. "How could it be," they ask, "that frail and perish-

able beings exalted themselves in this fashion?"
Those who are accustomed to thinking of man as a
"higher animal"; who have accepted the ultramundane
scientist's account of life's spontaneous origin and
progressive growth; who rely upon the psychological
explanation of the soul as nothing but a convenient
name for certain functions of the nervous system of
the body, are strongly disposed to place a question
mark, not only after the concept of immortality, but
also after the concept of the Supreme Being who is its
fountain.

Law, that magic word, is the solution of the problem. By it we must learn that we are nothing more
than machines of brief animation. Life's endowments
are no sooner consciously appreciated than they are
withdrawn. Yesterday we were, to-morrow we shall
not be. Let us seize the brittle thread so mysteriously
stretched between the abysses of birth, death and nothingness, and adjust ourselves as best we may to an
inevitable and pitiless doom. This for large groups of
men and women of our century is a sufficient theory
for the practice of well-ordered life. For still larger
groups it excites disillusion, despair and widespread
attempts to cheat so gloomy a fate by illicit pleasure
or sensual indulgence.

III

The interesting feature of this theory is that, while
esteemed by those who hold it as modern, scientific

and intellectually competent, it is an exceedingly
ancient, highly emotional and disappointing speculation. Contrary to prevalent supposition, the race in
its infancy did not postulate belief in immortality,
and then draw away from it because advancing intelligence negatived that belief. Such an assertion is remote from the facts. In every age some prophetic
spirits contended that life hereafter was the rational
outcome of life here, while the unbelieving rejected
the contention. Nearly every argument now urged
against immortality can be duplicated from the classic
thought of Greece. The Hebrew people originally
placed little or no credence in existence beyond the
grave. They visioned a shadowy underworld called
"Sheol" which loosely corresponded with the "Hades"
of pagan antiquity. But in their view it was in many
ways dissociated from the present world, and lay beyond the jurisdiction of their God Jehovah. Not a
few scholars insist that for primitive Judaism man was
a living whole, having the twofold aspect of body and
soul, and this is the view entertained by many to-day.
At death the soul does not proceed to a complete life
elsewhere, since without the body no such life is at-
tainable. What does persist after death is merely a
shade, concerning which the living show scanty interest.

Indeed, the chief concern of the early Hebrew was
for the continuity of his own family. What is now
termed "the corporate idea" pervaded his religious

ideas. He was either blessed or cursed in his posterity, who safeguarded him against oblivion. Happy was that Israelite whose wife was as a fruitful vine; the perpetuity of whose name was guaranteed by the number and worthiness of his sons and daughters.[1] At a later period "the corporate idea" was applied to the chosen nation. Was not the anticipated Messiah to reign over Israel's indissoluble commonwealth? Neither he nor it could fail or grow weary. Men may come and men may go, but the elect of God would go on forever. Out of this strong sense of social immortality faith in personal persistence ultimately emerged. It was a faith born of tragic experience. The collapse of the Jewish theocracy in the Exile compelled afflicted Israel to reconsider the entire question of God's purpose for His people. Superior spirits argued that since that purpose was one of redemptive grace and mercy, it would be realized whatever befell the chosen nation. Through this reappraisement the individual came into his own, and Jeremiah and Ezekiel boldly proclaimed immortality as his privilege by divine provision. Their correct evaluation of man met death's proud defiance with faith's answering challenge. In these prophets, in Psalms 73: 23-26 and 139: 7-12, and in Job 19: 25-27 some dim adumbrations of the Risen Christ's victory may be traced. They indicate that life is lord of death; that love shall never lose its own.

[1] Cf. Psalm 128: 3 ff.

IV

From this illumination Jewish conceptions of the future life took on a spiritual glow. It was expounded as a verity inherent in God's character and in that of His righteous servants. On the other hand, the way of the ungodly would perish. Why? Because they have no vital relations with a holy and just Deity. But this decided elevation of the doctrine of immortality was limited by the Hebrew's inability to think of life except as conditioned by the flesh. There had to be, as he saw the issue, a restoration of the body in order that full and perfect life may follow. At first, as in Ezekiel 37: 1-14 and Isaiah 26: 14, 19, only the bodies of Israel's righteous dead were to be restored. But by the second century before Christ a definite doctrine of universal resurrection had been formulated which included both good and evil doers.[1] The non-canonical apocryphal literature of this and later periods is rife with faith in that "Day of the Lord" when all the departed shall be summoned to His Judgment. In these vast hinterlands of the Christian Dispensation we may observe the gradual development under painful discipline of increasingly clear concepts of God's holy love, and of the unique value of human personality. These concepts were evolved into affirmative beliefs which in turn became sources of moral strength and religious enlightenment.

Did Jesus confirm those beliefs or must they stand

[1] Cf. Daniel 12: 12.

on their own merits as essential to life and conduct?
The answer should be absolutely determinative for
every Christian heart. I go further, and say that it
ought to be determinative for every person, Christian
or non-Christian, who concedes the principle that
"spiritual things are spiritually discerned." If the
"Strong Son of God" is not to be trusted on these high
matters of the soul, whom can we trust? If he was in
error here, what reasonable hope have we of getting
at the truth of any question outside the sphere of
scientific demonstration? Behind his forms of speech,
which were of necessity adapted to those he addressed,
was a divine consciousness of the eternities which
those forms have plowed into the soul of the world.
He incarnated that which he authorized. His su-
premacy consists in what he was even more than in
what he said or did. The complete consistency of his
perfect being revealed the truth that the Father's
grand design is the redemption of human personality,
and that all else is subordinate to this design. According to the Master's authority, everlasting life is
God's gift in Christ. That life he described as an
abiding consciousness of the Divine Presence; a life
begotten in every recipient and obedient spirit; a life
attested by definite experiences which nothing could
destroy. For the believer bodily dissolution thus became the soul's emancipation; the portal through
which he passed from life to more life; from peace
to deeper peace.

V

On the other hand, for those who rejected God's transcendent gift, death was the entrance to a life robbed of its divine aim; consigned to a poignant sense of increasing restriction and purposelessness, and tortured by an overwhelming awareness of incalculable loss. This interpretation of Christ's message harmonizes with his evangel as a whole, with what he was in himself, and with that quality of being and behavior which he alone creates in mankind. Again one asks, *"Was he right or wrong?"* Either life surpasses itself, vanquishes every carnal hindrance, and returns to its Source in the uncreate and all creating Father; or the "Prince of Life," as St. Peter entitled Jesus, was misled and misleading. It is generally admitted that he was life's unequaled exponent; that he stood on the topmost pinnacles of spiritual majesty and radiance. Yet how can the admission serve our profoundest needs if he erred concerning the truth about God and our essential being? His claim to be "The Light of the World," elsewhere sustained as it is by abundant evidence, is here invalidated. The Christian Church reasonably rejects so disastrous an alternative at the behest of those realities which must endure when all else shall suffer shock. Its answer to the query of the text, "If a man die, shall he live again?" is a convinced and changeless affirmative.

The singularly dogmatic assertions of contemporary scientists and thinkers of incipient or avowed agnosticism, that immortality is inconceivable, savors of intellectual insolence. A literary critic has recently said that the major Russian novelists insult humanity by attempting to deprive it of hope. What shall be said of experts learned in physical data who attempt to domineer over the indestructible instinct of the race that beyond its present range there is still more sea? Upon what rational basis do they assert that whatsoever in divine revelation taxes the mind or imagination must be disallowed? If we are to believe only the obvious; if we are not to believe the difficult, science itself is in a perilous state. It requires us to credit many phenomena which flatly contradict ordinary experience, and for which the evidence is wholly inferential.

The astronomer uses mathematics to measure magnitudes and distances which baffle even the keenest intelligence in the effort to apprehend them. Einstein's calculations have been lately spread in vain on the front pages of journalism. The large majority left them as they found them. Yet should some benighted cleric protest that he scorned Einstein's reckonings because the utmost use of imagination could not visualize the magnitudes and distances they involve, what a chorus of erudite rebuke he would evoke.

VI

Not a day dawns in which we are not invited to place credence in things by the side of which the belief that life outlasts death is simplicity itself. The fact that men who shy from immortality heartily indorse the evolutionary hypothesis seems to register in them a curious mental twist. They willingly agree that, while the planet has pursued its infinite cycles according to the fixed law of gravity, endless species of life and the several powers of its sentient existence have proceeded from a few original forms, or perchance from one form. They freely premise a world in which these forms actually existed in a suitable environment and with certain capacities. Yet when we ask for what end former death gave way to present life, their sole reply is in order that death may resume its former sway. They profess to find no difficulty in the claim of scientists that the non-living can evolve the living, the non-personal the personal, the non-moral the moral; in plain words, that the lesser produces the greater. But the Christian claim that the greater can perpetuate and remain itself despite bodily death, is regarded by them as a legendary superstition. It is not incredible that the unborn babe should become in time a Shakespeare or a Lincoln. It is incredible that the opulent imagination known as Shakespeare and the magnanimous spirit known as Lincoln should still be existent and active in the hereafter. Surely in this instance the incredulity belongs to the first rather than the second position. It is far less difficult to conceive personality persistent beyond death than to conceive personality's mysterious origin in life. Here the marvel is not immortality, but that life within man of which immortality is affirmed.

Again, in an era when the physical is emphasized at the expense of the spiritual, we do well to remind ourselves that the spiritual has repeatedly shown itself able to control the physical. We understand that the body must be if there is to be a soul. But we do not have to admit that the body is the predominant member of the partnership. If physical man is everything the athlete is his final achievement. But is he? Where shall we classify the saint, the prophet, the thinker, the scholar; the servants of the helpless who, notwithstanding crippled limbs and burdened frames, have lived valiantly and added to the aggregate of human good? Their fortitude in pain, their immolation of the flesh for the mind's ennoblement and for the heart's sacrificial ministry, cannot be relegated to the rear. The indubitable witness of experience will not have it so. Florence Nightingale outdid the Light Brigade in the Crimea, and one of her favorite authors, the Apostle St. Paul, although no candidate for the gladiator's arena, triumphed over the Roman Cæsars.

VII

The legend of "The Great Stone Face" illustrates the point. A secluded dweller in the valley beneath, by his constant contemplation of the features graven by Nature on the gigantic mountainside towering above, presently showed their benign strength in his own countenance. So do we gain the resemblance of that which we revere, and the transforming process is not at the beck and call of the grave. It cannot be accounted for on the supposition that men are as the "brute beasts that perish." Professor William James argues that so far from the brain being the condition of the spirit's existence, in all probability it is but its very imperfect medium, release from which would enable the spirit to move in a realm of action and experience otherwise impossible. Was it not Euripides who astonished a cynical pagan audience by suggesting that death might prove to be the commencement of another existence, in comparison with which the life we live here would be destitute indeed? Did not Socrates, with the deadly draught of hemlock at his lips, console his weeping friends by the assurance that "no evil can befall a good man either in this life or the next"?

But what of the jaded souls who do not crave immortality? "I do not want to live forever," is a fairly frequent remonstrance. Professor Leuba's questionnaire on "The Belief in God and Immortality" brought to light a considerable amount of this dissent. Others somewhat weary in the game of life are content to take what comes after death. Mrs. Huxley's lines on the tombstone of her famous husband express their attitude:

> Be not afraid, ye waiting hearts that weep;
> For still He giveth His beloved sleep:
> And if an endless sleep He wills, so best.

As one recalls that intrepid warrior for the scientifically verifiable, one is tempted to believe he is still pursuing his undaunted search for truth wherever truth is to be found in its final harmonies. Thus believing, one would rather say of him and all like him:

> Doubtless unto thee is given
> A life that bears immortal fruit
> In those great offices that suit
> The full grown energies of heaven.

VIII

It is not merely a matter, however, of what we *want*, but what we must actually *become*. None chooses to live in the first instance, and it is a permissible inference that none is empowered to choose whether he or she shall continue to live. Our boasted freedom has boundaries against which revolt is futile. Divine Sovereignty and the ultimatum of the Divine Will may be scouted by empirics, but experience does not vindicate their scorn. Our destiny is never in our own keeping. The Power not ourselves does not cry, nor cause its voice to be heard on the streets. Nevertheless we are forced to obey its edicts. It ordained our being, and if it so pleases it ordains our immortality.

Assuredly we know we live here and now, and that once we did not. But we do not know that we shall some day wholly cease to be. As against this guesswork, the affirmation of life's endlessness gives to man's present existence a solemn and moving significance it could not otherwise obtain. Biblical language is at its wit's end to depict the difference the sense of endlessness evokes in mortals. Above all else, it drives home the question: "What are we doing with life considered as an eternal possibility?"

A faulty reply has recently been revived and clarified in the idea of "social immortality." Its gist is connected with "the Religion of Humanity" founded by August Comte, and popularized by George Eliot, Harriet Martineau, John Stuart Mill and Frederic Harrison. Its tenets crop out in the somewhat extensive correspondence I receive from earnest and striving souls. They tell me that the one way of personality's continuance is by building it into the personalities of our fellow creatures. All other methods, as these later Positivists view them, are unintelligible.

Yet when scrutinized "social immortality" is a meaningless phrase. Granting the great benefit of elevating influence upon others, and with due regard for its proper place and functions, what has it to do with immortality itself? This signifies the deathlessness of the single personality. And the only conceivable way in which that deathlessness can be ours is by our retention of self-consciousness. To live on *in* others, but not to be aware of it ourselves, is at the polarities from Christ's teaching about immortality. In truth, on his authority, it is not to live at all.

IX

Since character is a personal quality, it depends on the continuity of the person whose character it is. Any given quality must be quality of someone or something. Moreover, this alleged social immortality is destined to vanish. The individual, we are told, survives only in society, and therein his values or disvalues are conserved. But how can this be unless the process is endless? And how can the process be endless since all strictly earthly existence is mortal? There was a time when this planet could not support life and a similar time will come again. When it does Comte's hypothesis must necessarily vanish.

We cannot entertain the denial of individual immortality because the denial destroys the faith necessary to good life. The prospect of an unavoidable desolation in which all for which the race has struggled and died shall be as though it had never been, appalls the reflecting mind. The last word of materialism and naturalism is one of unmitigated pessimism. On the other hand, the consciousness of personal immortality lifts man up forever. It constitutes him a pilgrim of the infinite. It convinces him that "the law of the harvest" is not confined to the here and now. It demonstrates that a momentous fate attaches to every human soul. It admonishes him that his equipment of attitude, habit and purpose, whether for good or ill, must decide his fitness for the hereafter. A truce, however, to these reasonings, which are only offered because they may be more conducive to our renewed trust in the God of eternal life than rhetorical portrayals of a paradise adorned with the gorgeous imageries of the Orient.

THE CERTITUDE OF IMMORTALITY

X

The gravamen of this discussion in an age of doubt centers around the Risen Living Christ. I fall back with you upon his revelation and upon the vital difference made by our acceptance or rejection of that revelation. I believe with faith unfeigned in him and in his power to bestow eternal life on all who by patient continuance in well-doing shall be counted worthy of his inexpressible gift. Do we not want him to be right? Whatever our doubts and fears, shall we not cling to his omnipotent love?

Think of those who looked to him and were delivered from their bondage; Thomas Arnold of Rugby is a case in point. He constrained his gifted son Matthew to believe that his father could not die. That son visited his father's tomb in Rugby chapel, and knew *he was not there*. In memorable lines he thus apostrophized that father:

> O strong soul, by what shore
> Tarriest thou now? For that force,
> Surely, has not been left vain!
> Somewhere, surely, afar,
> In the sounding labour-house vast
> Of being, is practised that strength,
> Zealous, beneficent, firm!
>
> Yes, in some far shining sphere,
> Conscious or not of the past,
> Still thou performest the word
> Of the Spirit in whom thou dost live—
> Prompt, unwearied as here!

Still thou upraisest with zeal
The humble good from the ground,
Sternly repressest the bad!
Still, like a trumpet, dost rouse
Those who with half-open eyes
Tread the border-land dim
'Twixt vice and virtue; reviv'st
Succourest!—this was thy work,
This was thy life upon earth.

If these are not true sentiments, what a mockery the human heart's loftiest impulses are! But the Risen Living Christ verifies them. If he has not satisfied man's quest for life, if all he ever was molders in a Syrian grave and nothing is left of him but dust and ashes, the darkness that falls on the human race is impenetrable; the riddle of its existence is insoluble; and death, reversing Nature's order here, tyrannizes over life hereafter. Men will not have it so. Deep calls unto deep again in them. St. Paul said, "The death that he died, he died unto sin once; but the life that he liveth, he liveth unto God." Disbelieve these words, and human life has no adequate explanation and admits of none. Believe them, and you also shall live, in the coherent, meaningful challenging life of the Spirit, having its dynamic for persistence and the promise of its triumph, in the Risen and Eternal Christ.

Immortality as Sure as God Himself

GEORGE COLEMAN, LL.D.

Mr. George Coleman, in spite of the fact that he is a layman, and, as such, was requested to write the sermon on Immortality representing the laymen, has managed to annex to himself several degrees including an LL.D. from Colby College, which was conferred upon him in 1911. He was born in Boston June 16th, 1867, and graduated with the famous Franklin Medal from the English High School in Boston.

He has been closely identified with the religious journalism of Boston, particularly with the Christian Endeavor World as business manager, but in recent years has become known from coast to coast through his executive leadership of the famous Ford Hall Open Forum, which has been known for a quarter of a century as the freest forum in America.

He has been for years President of the Annual Sociological Conferences at Sagamore Beach, a member of the Boston City Council, President of the Northern Baptist Convention 1917-18 and now President of the Babson Institute, Wellesley Hills,

Mass. He is the author of innumerable articles on church and business
and of several books, including
Searchlights, The People's Prayers
and *Democracy in the Making.*

Immortality as Sure as God Himself

By GEORGE W. COLEMAN, PRESIDENT, BABSON INSTITUTE, CHAIRMAN, FORD HALL FORUM

BY NATURE I am always questioning things. Everything, almost without exception, must undergo critical examination if I have any interest in it at all. I was brought up in the Christian faith. During intellectual adolescence I revolted. It took me years to think my way back and I never did arrive at the place where I started. And now for twenty years and more through the activities of the Open Forum I have trained myself to look tolerantly at both sides of all great questions. How well I remember that night more than fifteen years ago when the great Lyman Abbott expounded to a crowded Ford Hall Forum audience largely of unbelievers his own abiding faith in personal immortality. The crowd was very respectful and highly appreciative but not by any means fully persuaded.

There were those in that audience who were in violent opposition to everything authoritative in religion. There were those who had discarded everything supernatural. There were those yearning for some satisfying proof that we shall live again. A few were there who would be quite content, if not happy, to pass out into oblivion. Some had no desire for personal immortality and believed their spirits would flow back into the life of God as the raindrops flow back through the rivers into the mighty ocean. And some there were who fervently shared the faith of the great scholar, preacher and editor who was addressing them. Familiar reactions, all of these attitudes, to an age-long question.

That address made an indelible impression on me but since that time psychology has raised some challenging questions and the proof then adduced does not seem to hold as strongly as it did then. But the quest is as keen as ever. After a full rich life of three score years and with the certainty of a relatively short run to the end, how does it all look to me now? What has life taught me as to another world? Can an honest, questioning mind rest happily in the faith that characterizes almost all religions? Is there good and sufficient reason for going contrary to the generally accepted belief of an overwhelming proportion of mankind all the way down through the centuries?

It can be argued that the Old Testament laid little stress on the future life and the Jews even today reverse the Christian emphasis and stress righteous life on this earth, leaving the next world in God's hands. Christians have been prone to fall into the error of otherworldliness to the neglect of the life here and now. It is staggering to the imagination to contemplate the countless billions of human beings in all stages of development who have made their home on this planet since the advent of man. But it is just as blinding to view the firmament and try to think of other universes millions and trillions of light-years distant. There is plenty of room in God's creation. And either one of these thoughts will suggest to a humble man that there are immense and significant *facts* utterly beyond his ken. There are those who assume to believe only that which can be attested through the five senses, and measured with material instruments. But they do not really mean that any more than do those men at the opposite end of the pole who insist that they believe every word in the Bible. You cannot X-ray love, hate, envy or devotion nor locate them in the human economy but there is nothing more real and powerful.

Hungry hearts and restless minds cry out in despair if only some one would return from the dead and tell us about it; then indeed would we believe and rejoice. We could not, we would not believe if one returned from the grave. We would doubt our own physical senses and everyone else would doubt us until we would become completely bewildered. There are thousands upon thousands who today sincerely believe that they have seen and conversed with departed spirits. But most of us pay little attention to it and give it no credence whatsoever. Are we so built that we could comprehend such an experience if it did actually happen to us? I spent an evening in Boston at one of the famous Margery séances. While the demonstration was mystifying to a high degree I came away a rather emphatic doubting Thomas. And just now as I am writing we are all stirred up by an amazing article in a popular magazine entitled "Seven Minutes in Eternity." The author of that article had his whole life completely changed for the better by a vividly realizing sense of having spent seven to ten minutes on the other side of the veil. And I must confess that Bill Pelley's mental experience, even if that is all it was, impresses me far more than the manipulation of material things by unseen forces in a "dim" but not "religious" light.

While almost everybody in his heart of hearts believes in immortality almost everybody wants to believe in it just a little more than he does. And then there are those who would give anything to be able to believe in it but they cannot, try as hard as they will. That is the state of one who is near and dear to me and I can't seem to help any. And two of my closest friends, mother and daughter, lived and died nobly and serenely without ever desiring personal survival. That was a staggering experience to me at the time but I think I have thought it through.

In the Scriptures I find in two brief statements the age-long quest of the human soul and the complete and only answer there is to that cry. Each expression stands on its own merit without the need of any support from divine inspiration. One's own heart and

44

head furnish the only confirmation that is necessary. Was it not Job who expressed the question that lies at the bottom of every man's heart, "If a man die, shall he live again?" And that is exactly what we all want to know. After a fairly long life of intense activity and wide contacts, facing death and seeing death repeatedly, with a heart full of longings unsatisfied and a head full of questionings unanswered, I find complete satisfaction in the declaration, "Shall not the Judge of all the earth do right?" Here in ten words, in so far as I am concerned, is the sum and substance of the whole business. Your own idea of God will determine for you what it would be right for Him to do as to a future life.

To believe in God at all is a pure act of faith. It can be reasoned out but it cannot be proved or disproved. I have earnest and noble friends who call themselves atheists but I have always found on close examination that they are disbelievers in some false God, some misconception of God in whom I disbelieve as heartily as they. To my mind it is the very height of credulity to deny the existence of God, nay more, it is the altogether unthinkable when pressed to its logical conclusion. I can understand the position of the agnostic who finds that he cannot think it through but I cannot understand the position of the atheist because he does not think it through.

But perhaps you are saying "why discuss God when your theme is Immortality?" Because the latter is but the corollary of the former; if there is no God, then there is no immortality, no anything but a meaningless whirligig of time. Taking God for granted we must necessarily conclude that a moral God must have a perfect law of compensation. There must be justice for the individual unless we utterly mistake Him. Few there be who feel that they have had perfect justice in this life. Most of us feel that we could do much better under more favorable conditions. Even those who have made the best of this life feel that they have only just begun and could go on to still higher development in another world. Immortality becomes an essential belief when we think of those who have had little or no chance in this world. And how about those cut off in their youth, our millions of young soldiers? Death is so often a frustration, something fine and great not realized. And what shall we think of that inspiring, indomitable soul, Helen Keller, deaf, dumb and blind from her youth up? Is she never to be freed from those handicaps? However complacent we may be for ourselves as to a future life, how can we entertain the thought that a moral God will not have compensations in another world for Helen Keller and millions still more unfortunate? However modest and humble we may feel as to the value of extending our own lives, what must be our thoughts for others whom we greatly admire and highly esteem, especially when they are cut off prematurely?

No, no, life cannot rest in a negation. We are in

46

a dynamic not a static universe. Life not death is in the saddle. Personality, identifiable and recognizable, the most precious thing we know, must share with all the rest. It will change but it will not disappear. Matter itself is only a form of electrical energy. Everything changes form but nothing is lost. In very recent years our horizons of knowledge have been enormously extended. At the same time our powers of control over nature have been vastly multiplied. If we can succeed in matching these accomplishments with commensurate growth in the mastery over our own human nature we will be well on our way toward a transformation of life that may bring us to the very threshold of the world beyond and enable us to get glimpses of the life within such as will not only satisfy our age-long yearnings and answer our impossible questions, but will also open up to us new mysteries which it has not yet entered into the heart of man even to imagine.

Personal immortality is as sure as God himself. I have tried to preach my sermon from the point of view of any man who believes in God regardless of his religious affiliations or the lack of them. For myself, I would not be forlorn nor without a grand and glorious hope and expectation if such belief were all I had to depend on. Somehow or other in spite of everything I have been led to trust God and to trust him supremely, above every principality and power, above life and death, above every church and creed and above all scriptures. While that anchor will always hold fast, I know full well my idea of God has come to me through the life of Jesus of Nazareth. And what he is reported to have said and done two thousand years ago in Palestine is balm to my soul, a strengthening to my faith, a comradeship in the walk of life and an expectation for the life beyond.

Immortality and the Comforter

HENRY HITT CRANE

Henry Hitt Crane was born in Danville, Ill., Feb. 2nd, 1890.

His father was a Methodist minister, and one of his last pastorates was in Peoples Temple, Boston, Mass. Here this young minister-to-be got his city background; here he learned to love Boston and New England, which later gave him a place in its heart such as only his own father had found in a preceding generation.

Dr. Crane graduated from Wesleyan Conn. in 1913 and received an S.T.B. degree from Boston University School of Theology in 1916, being given the honorary degree of D.D. by DePauw University in 1921. He was a member of Delta Tau Delta Fraternity, is a Mason and an Odd Fellow.

He has served several churches in New England, his longest ministry being at Malden Center Methodist Episcopal Church, where he preached to crowded congregations for nine years, in addition to a lecture schedule which took him all over the Eastern United States. He has for years been particularly popular as an Evangelist to college students.

Youthful in appearance, genial, friendly, warm-hearted, with a captivating smile, Henry Hitt Crane has been justly characterized as one of the most popular preachers in all New England.

During the past year he was called to the famous Elm Park Methodist Episcopal Church in Scranton, Pennsylvania, one of the truly great churches of Methodism, where he has opened an unusual ministry, already attracting state wide attention.

As one of the younger voices of the church world we are glad to have him contribute this sermon on Immortality.

Immortality and the Comforter

By Henry H. Crane

"If a man die, shall he live again?"
—JOB XIV: 14
"If it were not so, I would have told you."
—JOHN XIV: 2

PERHAPS the oldest and most persistent question of the human heart is that of the immortality of the soul, the persistence of personality beyond the grave. There seems never to have been a time when mankind was not considering it. Job was not the first person to articulate the ancient query; nor was he the last. When Eve sat staring, stony-eyed, into the aching void, with the head of her dead boy in her lap, she doubtless let fall from her lips the same agonizing, insistent soul-cry which ever since has been repeated by innumerable multitudes: "If a man die, shall he live again?"

Today, as yesterday, the answers given to this age-old question are of three general types. In the first place, there is the denial of the doubter. In the absence of any actual knowledge as to the reality of immortality such a person insists that he cannot feel that the preponderance of probability is sufficient to justify belief in the theory. Because there is no such evidence as would demonstrate beyond peradventure of a doubt that there is life beyond the grave, because all the efforts of science to produce proofs have been unsuccessful, because certain facts of life seem to contradict the idea, he doubts the validity of the belief altogether. Such a man was Thomas Huxley, for example. He insisted that he could not give assent to the theory. To this heroic champion of modern science there did not seem to be sufficient evidence of the sort he sought to warrant his acceptance of the idea. Even when he stood by the grave of his oldest child, Noel, overwhelmed with grief, and his great-hearted friend, Charles Kingsley, besought him to find comfort in the immortal hope, Mr. Huxley replied, "I have searched over the ground of my belief, and if wife and child and name and fame were all to be lost to me one after the other as the penalty, still I would not lie." Such an attitude has been shared by men of all ages—an attitude of virtual denial born of an honest doubt.

In the second place, there is the answer of indifference. Always there have been those who are simply not concerned with the question of immortality for the reason that they deem the whole issue quite inconsequential. These are they who ask, whenever the matter comes up, "What of it? What difference does it make one way or another?" The reasons for this attitude are not difficult to discover, and at first blush they appear to be quite impressive. Here, for example, are men who are face to face with daily duties, challenging tasks and captivating opportunities. Life to them is most engaging. "Why think of what lies beyond?" they ask. "To dream of the hereafter dampens one's ardor to work while here. Let each man do his duty today and not worry about tomorrow. If life continues after death, well and good; if not, no matter. There may not, indeed, be any immortality for the individual soul. Think then of the immortality of influence one may achieve. Work not for your own soul's sake, but for humanity's sake. Live such a life as will make the world a better place for your children to live in. Hand down to the next generation a heritage of happiness, no matter what may happen to you. 'Take no thought of the morrow,' " they quote. " 'Sufficient unto the day is the evil thereof.' "

Such an answer to the question of immortality is not to be ignored, for it springs not from a lazy unconcern about vital matters, but from an excessive emphasis, perhaps, on what appear to be the immediate practicalities. Before passing, therefore, to the consideration of the third type of answer—that of the triumphant believer; and before attempting to give the deepest reasons we can think of for belief in the persistence of personality (which is the main purpose of this sermon), let us ask briefly just what difference it *does* make whether we believe in immortality.

To cite a single aspect of the problem as illustrative of others, it might be wise to consider the mighty difference the belief in immortality makes in the way

we think of *ourselves*. What *are* we, really: animal or
spirit, mud or mind, body or soul? If the former,
then we may have our little day and cease to be—and
obviously it doesn't matter much what one believes
about life after death; indeed, the idea of immortality
resolves itself into an absurdity. If, however, we are
in reality the latter—spirit, mind, soul—then it would
seem that nothing short of eternity would suffice for
the development of our spiritual potentialities.

What more significant item could there be in esti-
mating the dignity of the human soul than this matter
of immortality? It makes all the difference between
vanity and priceless value whether we are to run our
course in a few days, or whether we are to go on forever in an ascending pathway of development. Immortality is thus the ultimate assertion of supreme
spiritual value in man.

Let a person come to believe that so far as he is
concerned all is over when death smites him, and how
shall you convince him that it is worth while to struggle on in the face of adversity, disappointment and
defeat? To be sure, as long as the sun shines and
fortune favors we shall be glad to live on "for the
sake of humanity"; but when the dark clouds of dis-
aster and despair settle down about us, what more rational gesture could there be than simply "to cock your
revolver and die"?

There has been considerable speculation concerning
the epidemic of student suicides. It seems fairly
simple to explain when one realizes what some of these

youngsters have been taught to believe, namely, that after all they are but a "chance collocation of atoms," a mere cleverly devised mechanism. If that, then what's the use of continuing to be when being has become burdensome? Let us dissolve the atoms, or stop the mechanism and—well, what difference does it make?

On the other hand, let a man believe that he is an abiding spirit; then come what may—sunshine or storm, delight or defeat, success or sorrow—it is all but a discipline for the soul. He stands magnificently undisturbed, unscathed and unembittered. The struggle is altogether worth while for there are eternal results! It does make a difference—this belief in immortality!

It is because of this fact that there has always been a third class—those whom I would call the triumphant believers! Their answer to the age-old question, "If a man die, shall he live again?" is a mighty affirmative. But it is the affirmative of a rational faith, not of a blind belief, nor yet of demonstrable knowledge.

We are forever asking how we can *know* that death does not end all, that if a man die he shall live again. Frankly, I do not think we can "know" in the sense that it can be proven or actually demonstrated, as one would prove a mathematical proposition or some scientific theory. As Martineau remarked, "We do not believe in immortality because we can prove it, but we try to prove it because we cannot help believing it." In other words, the ultimate argument for life after death is the *instinct* of the human soul. "When God wants to carry a point with His children," says Emerson, "He plants His arguments in the instincts." This, it seems to me, is what Jesus recognized when he met this great issue of immortality with that singularly simple but suggestive statement I have chosen for our second text: "If it were not so, I would have told you." By these words the Master sought to place our confidence in the persistence of personality, not upon some dogmatic utterance about which men might quarrel, but right upon the deepest instincts of humanity; which instincts, in the last analysis, are far better than any mere "head knowledge."

We *know*, really, only the lower things of life. The best things of life we *feel*. We know that two and two make four; we can prove that. We know that the shortest distance between two points is a straight line; that is axiomatic—by which we mean that it is so clear that there is nothing clearer by which we can prove it. But what if we *can* prove these statements? Can a man live on such dead ideas? Even after they have been proven, what of it? They don't matter much, so far as life is concerned. But take such a thing as Love, for example—a matter of life and death, if you please. One never *knows* that another loves him, in the sense that it can be proven beyond peradventure of a doubt so as to convince a mind disposed to believe otherwise. Or take Honor or Integrity. We never *know* that it pays to be true and honest and strong and noble and pure. All these things are not of knowledge. They

56

are convictions; they are instincts of the soul. And here, among these instincts, is the deepest argument for immortality—which is just what Jesus divined and directed us to when he said: "If it were not so, I would have told you."

Let us look, then, at some of these instincts; and directly, if I mistake not, we shall see how utterly impossible it would be for a good and wise God to allow this human career to cease at the grave.

In the first place, every man is full of *desires*—and the broader and deeper and better the man, the more and greater his desires. Civilization, considered in its wider sense, is but the development of new desires and new ways of gratifying them. Education is but the transforming of low desires into higher, more intellectual, more spiritual desires. Then note this: *The better a man's desires in this life, the less probability is there of their gratification!*

Is it not strange that there is such an anomaly, such an irregularity in nature? The fish has no desire that the water about it cannot gratify. When God made a wing, he made air against which that wing was to beat. Nowhere in nature will you find any half-hinges; nowhere in the lower order of creation will you find any desires unless in the environment of the creature there is provided that which can satisfy the desire;—nowhere *except in man*. And my desires! The whole earth cannot meet them. I desire money. Give it to me, all that I can keep and hold, and doubtless, the more I have the more restless I will become. I desire wisdom. Let me be the wisest of all men, and like the wisest of all men I will sit down and write my testimony: "Vanity of vanities; all is vanity and vexation of spirit." Let me desire love. I can only hold love for a few brief years. Somewhere comes the grave to cut it off. If God made man to live only this earthly life, then he made a Frankenstein, a monster who only exists to reproach Him.

And what of the *elusiveness of life?* The poet says that man never is, but always to be blest. We live by hope. We enjoy anticipation. The realization has always some tiny tinge of disappointment in it. The boy thinks he will be happy when he gets to college, and at college all his dreams are of what he will do when he gets through. And when he gets out into the world of business or of his chosen profession, he is always looking forward to the success he shall accomplish. And when he accomplishes his success—nine-tenths of them don't accomplish it—but when the one does, he is looking forward still to something, and old age finds him with his back bowed and his hair silvered, still looking forward. Truly we are but pilgrims and strangers here. Why did the Maker create this race of beings to be lured on and on by something held before them, only to drop them at last into annihilation? If it were not so that this immortal spirit shall live on to find these hopes at last come into reality, He would have told us.

And then, if this life be all, look how all discipline is wasted. We spend forty, fifty, sixty years, learning how to live. A man just learns how to live and then he dies. "Oh," you say, "if I had had the discipline when I was twenty that I have now that I am sixty, how much better I might have done; how many follies I might have omitted; how many mistakes I might have avoided! But now that I have accumulated my discipline, the vital sap has run out, and the strength of life has disappeared." Would you do so with your son? Would you carefully train your boy to be a mechanic or an engineer or an orator or a writer or a business man, and then, just as he graduates from college, take him off and kill him? And would God Almighty train men, the best of men, by the discipline of a long life, until they are more nearly able and competent to do and to think properly, and then drop them into oblivion? A cruel God might; but no Father, such as my Christ revealed, would do this. For the great beyond we live and learn. We realize There what we long for here. *If it were not so, He would have told us!*

Look, too, at the highest faculties you have, the faculties that you feel to be the noblest within you. The more remote a man's aims, the nobler his life. Do you mean to tell me that man, giving himself up to all fleshly and sensual aims, that man who cares nothing for noble purposes and high thought, groveling in gross gratification, yet living just decently enough to keep out of the penitentiary and avoid social complications —do you mean to tell me that monster is reaching the real goal of life, rather than you who are perpetually disciplining yourself to a nobler aim?

And what of our sense of *justice?* We believe in justice, but how little justice there is here. We see a lying politician or a prestigious physician or an unscrupulous lawyer or a "lawful" swindler living proudly in a fine house, with his magnificent equipage, insolently enjoying all the so-called fruits and pleasures of earth—we see these constantly about us, while many an honest man toils terribly and is denied even a living wage or a fair opportunity for betterment, say nothing of the constant denial of the best there is for him. Is that just, and will a kind and wise and good God allow that to be the permanent order of things? No, if it were not so that there was another life in which this injustice can be righted, He would have told us.

Then mark a deeper instinct in man, the deepest instinct of all, the love of life, that you can never get out of any human being. The beggar has it; no matter how wretched his existence, and how desperately he must live, he still wants to live. A man sentenced for life in the penitentiary still clings to life. The invalid who has spent years in disease and suffering still wants the physician to use every means to enable him to hang on a little longer.

> Gnaw my withers, wrack my bones,
> Life, mere life, for all atones.

We call this the first law of nature—life! *Eternal* life! Could the language of this instinct mean anything else? Eternal life—there must be! Is it not so, oh Christ? And he says, as of old, "If all the deep instincts of your being were to be blasted, I would have told you."

And then the Bible! Look into it. We say it is a book of promises. Yet none of these promises has been fully kept. And if there be no immortality then "we are of all men most miserable." Go back into the Old Testament. Abraham was promised the promised land. He never got it. His children never got it all; they had it but partially. Moses was promised this land. The nearest he got to it was when he stood on the top of the mountain and saw its prospect; his foot never pressed it. "All these," says the Apostle, "died, not having received the promise." The early church expected Christ to return bodily; he never came. We have always been looking forward to the fulfillment of these things literally. They have never been fulfilled.

So in our own case. This Book promises us that Jesus shall save us from sin. Have any of us been saved from sin absolutely? No, we have been saved in a measure, but only in a measure. The perfect salvation does not come in this life. He has promised to justify us, to make us just. Has that perfect justness ever come? He has promised to adopt us into his family and make us sons of God. Have we ever felt we were worthy of calling ourselves sons of God in very truth? We only use this language when we take

61

into consideration what we shall be. He has said, "Come unto me, and I will give you rest." Have we ever received a perfect rest? Not perfect. Perfect joy? Always some bitterness in the cup. Perfect satisfaction? We shall never be satisfied until we awake in his likeness.

And so I come to the gates of death with all these fragmentary promises of my instincts in my hands; I come with these half-promises of the Bible, still unfulfilled, in my hands—I come to the gate of death, and by these very unfulfilled promises demand of my Maker that there be another life in which my life shall be rounded, another life in which I shall attain the ends for which I have been made. And at the gate of death I hear the word of my Christ again: *If it were not so, I would have told you.*

Yes, truly, man is the anomaly of all nature. The horse and the cow are satisfied with their food and their pasture. Man alone is unsatisfied. The human soul—you could put it into the kingdoms of the earth and all the galaxies of the stars, and it would still cry out for more. Why is this anomaly?

You have heard the story of the ugly duckling? All the ducks in the barnyard made sport of this little awkward stranger. He couldn't walk as they did; his neck was too long and his wings were too clumsy. So all during his duckhood he had to spend his life the scorn of his companions; until one spring day, when the air was balmy and soft, and they heard above them a strange and distant sound as of birds flying and crying, this ugly duckling looked up and saw a little speck in the sky, and then a waving line, and from that line there came the call to him. He tried his wings, he spread them and then he sprang from the ground and soared into the air, and his companions knew him no more. He did not belong to them. And, by the way, I think they said he had *died*.

Go down to a city by the side of the sea. You see there many houses around you, houses with pointed roofs and flat bottoms, all made to sit upon the ground, and then suddenly you come to another house, turned the other way. The point is at the bottom and the flat part is on the top. It will not stand alone; it has to be propped up. It is not made to sit upon the ground. How strangely out of place it seems! But wait until the day of launching comes; take away the props and it slides out into the sparkling waters of the sea and floats gracefully among the waves. That was not made for the earth, but for the mighty ocean.

And so when I look at people, and at myself—dissatisfied, restless, uneasy, surrounded by unideal conditions, body, soul, and heart crying out for the unattained; I say this is not our permanent abiding-place. Just as surely as the God that made things knew how to make them, some day the call will come to you and you shall try your wings and fly to where God has made a home for you. For "In my Father's house are many mansions: if it were not so, I would have told you."

Immortality and Eternal Life

HARRY EMERSON FOSDICK
D.D., LL.D.

Harry Emerson Fosdick was born in Buffalo, N. Y., May 24th, 1878, and was graduated from Colgate University in 1900, receiving a D.D. from the same school in 1914 and a B.D. from Union Theological Seminary in 1904. He has received degrees from Columbia, Yale, Princeton, Brown, the University of Michigan, Ohio State, the University of Rochester, and others.

He was ordained into the Baptist Ministry in 1903 and was pastor of the first Baptist Church in Montclair, N. J., from 1904 to 1915, and instructor in Homiletics at Union Theological Seminary from 1908 to 1915. He has been professor of Practical Theology at Union since 1915. He is minister of the Riverside Church in New York City, the beautiful, new cathedral adjoining the campus of Columbia University.

Dr. Fosdick is widely known as the author of a series of little books which have been circulated throughout the world in hundreds of editions: *The Manhood of the Master, The Meaning of Prayer, The Meaning of Faith, The Meaning of Service.* His other volumes are *Twelve Tests of Character, The Modern Use of the Bible, A Pilgrimage to Palestine, Adventurous Religion,* etc.

The present sermon was Dr. Fosdick's 1929 Easter message in the Park Avenue Baptist Church.

Immortality and Eternal Life

By HARRY EMERSON FOSDICK

"This is life eternal, that they might know thee the only true God, and Jesus Christ, whom thou hast sent."

—JOHN XVII: 3

LET us begin our thought by noting that Easter is not simply Christian. It does not come alone from that little band of disciples in Jerusalem who, dismayed by the crucifixion of their Lord, were re-created by their confidence that Jesus was alive. Easter in the early centuries gathered up also elements from the pre-Christian mystery religions with their dying and their rising lords, Adonis, and the rest, in whose trouble and triumph, defeat and victory, multitudes before Christ had symbolized their experience. And in subsequent centuries Easter has gathered up the spring festivals of Northern Europe, where our barbarian forefathers long had celebrated nature's victory over winter's death. The Easter festival, as we have it now, is a river into which many streams have poured their contributions.

That is to say, the experience which we celebrate today is deeply, significantly human. Good Friday and Easter, defeat and victory, trouble and triumph, death and immortality—every human being finds his problem symbolized in Easter day.

As the years pass, one finds that life tends to become either meaningless or meaningful, and no preacher is needed to point out that, so far as happiness is concerned, that difference is profoundly significant. Deeper than the contrast between wealth and poverty, deeper than the contrast between education and the lack of it is this: as the years progress does life grow meaningless or meaningful?

Let us visualize this contrast in the experience of two men who have left their record for us in the Scriptures. On the one side, the author of the book of Ecclesiastes found life growing meaningless. "That which befalleth the sons of men," he says, "befalleth beasts. The same to both. As the one dieth, so dieth the other; yea, they have all one breath; so that a man hath no preëminence above a beast: for all is foolishness." And on the other side, the author of the Fourth Gospel finds his life growing meaningful. "This is life eternal, that they might know thee the only true God, and Jesus Christ, whom thou hast sent."

On Easter morning we ask ourselves which of these two represents the drift of our experience: "all is foolishness," or "this is life eternal."

Note the meaning of that phrase "life eternal." It does not primarily denote something after death. It primarily denotes a kind of life which we may live now. "This is life eternal, that they might know thee the only true God, and Jesus Christ, whom thou hast sent." But to know God and Christ is something that a man can begin now. Eternal life is not simply post-mortem: it is also a present possession. Always distinguish, therefore, between immortality and eternal life. Immortality is merely going on and on. Eternal life is having a kind of life so radiant in meaning that it is worth going on with. Immortality is mere continuance of existence. Eternal life is quality of experience.

Whenever in the New Testament, therefore, you find eternal life mentioned, it always involves present possession as a possibility. "He that hath the Son hath life." He hath "passed from death unto life." It is in us now "a well of water springing up into everlasting life." "This is life eternal, that they might know thee." Always in the New Testament eternal life begins here.

Of course, immortality without eternal life, so far from being desirable, is terrible. One stands in amazement before some folk apparently hungry for mere continuance of existence beyond death, as though, after all, this were a thing to be desired. The Buddhists, on the contrary, are in so far right, that having to go on and on in what they call the wheel of re-birth, never being able to stop going on, no knife keen enough to cut the cord, no poison strong enough to dissolve the bondage, is by itself the most appalling conception that ever haunted the imagination of man. No wonder that the orthodox Buddhist doctrine of salvation springs from a passionate desire to escape from immortality! There is only one condition under which *immortality* ever can be desirable: namely, that a man have *eternal life*, the kind of life, the quality of experience, so full of meaning that it makes going on worth while. The basic difficulty with Buddhism is that while it started with immortality, it shrank back because it did not have the idea which in the New Testament is called "eternal life."

This contrast clears up the difficulty that so many people have about Jesus' contribution in this realm. Many folk seem to think that because the New Testament says that Christ bestowed eternal life on his disciples, it means that he bestowed immortality. "But that would be nonsense," they say. "Men believed in immortality long before Jesus came. Read Plato's *Phædo*, for one of the most glorious statements of faith in immortality ever written. Christ did not give men immortality." To which, of course, the answer is plain. To be sure, he did not. Who said he did? What the New Testament says is that Christ led men into eternal life. That is not identical with immortality. That means that Christ led his disciples into a quality of experience so rich and radiant that it was worth going on with.

Moreover, the practical upshot of this distinction is clear. Quit postponing eternal life! Now is the time to go to heaven. Do not wait. As a Scotch Christian said, "That is where I am living now." Those first disciples entered into eternal life in ancient Palestine

—a most unlikely place. We can enter into it in New York City just as easily. Eternal life begins here.

Do you remember that phrase, half slang, which in our youth we used when joy ran high? "This is the life!" we said. In a great sense the New Testament is always saying that. This is the life. "The life which is life indeed," they called it, and in the center of the book stood One who cried, "I am come that they might have life, and that they might have it more abundantly." In contrast with that radiant and tingling experience how different is the voice that says, "Man hath no preëminence above a beast: for all is foolishness."

Note, further, that as between these two attitudes toward life we are bound to drift one way or the other. We cannot avoid that. As the years pass, the events of life inevitably accumulate intellectual interpretations and emotional reactions. The differences between us do not lie primarily in what happens to us. Pretty nearly everything happens to most of us. Good fortune and bad fortune, success and failure, trouble and triumph, health and sickness, love and death— most things happen to most of us. The differences between us do not mainly consist in the experiences we undergo but in what we inwardly do with them by our interpretations and reactions.

Trouble comes to two men. Listen to them. One says, "Our light affliction, which is but for a moment, worketh for us a far more exceeding and eternal weight of glory; while we look not at the things which are

seen, but at the things which are not seen." That is
Paul. The other one says that He must have been an
ill-advised God who could find no better sport than
to change Himself into so hungry a world. That is
Schopenhauer. Now, the difference between Paul and
Schopenhauer is not mainly in what happened to them.
Some very fortunate and some very terrific things happened to both of them. The difference lies in what
they did with them, in their interpretations and reactions.

Or, here are two men looking at mankind with all
its good and evil. Says John, "Now are we the sons
of God, and it doth not yet appear what we shall be."
A modern novelist says that man "is only a bundle of
cellular matter upon its way to become manure." The
difference between those two men does not lie primarily
in what happened to them but in what they did to it
with their interpretations and reactions. In the long
run, therefore, life does not so much make us as we
make life by what we do with it. Inevitably we drift
one way or the other: "all is foolishness" or "this is
life eternal."

So often I talk directly to young people that they
may forgive me this morning for talking about something that probably does not directly hit their present
experience. I mean that young people naturally get
their consciousness that life is worth while out of
present pleasures. The first time I heard a comic
opera I felt a thrill that lasted me a week. My first
impression was that if I could hear a comic opera every

night I should be entirely happy. That is natural. Youth characteristically gets its satisfactions out of immediacies. But an observing older man can tell youths what is going to happen to them: that as they grow in age, they are going to become progressively aware of an accumulating mass of interpretations and reactions, that gather momentum, that gain ascendency, that dominate the direction and control the quality of their living, and in the end in one degree or another they are going to find themselves saying about life either "all is foolishness" or else "this is life eternal." Even at an early stage of their development they may well recognize that the first, the sense of futility and meaninglessness in life, is hell, and the second, that life is rich in meaning, is happiness.

Which leads us, as you see, straight into the question: what is the real road to happiness after all? One looks out across a city like New York, and the dominant impression is of millions of people trying desperately hard to be happy. One passes thousands of them on the street with deep chasms of difference between them in every item of outward circumstance or inward attitude, but all of them having this thing true: they want to be happy.

Well, we want them to be happy but if even on such a day as our festival of victory over death we should go to the generality of them and say, "Come, be Christians and be happy!" that would seem absurd to them. "Be Christians," they would say, "to be happy! Christianity does not make people happy.

73

Think of all the intolerance, the bitterness, the strife that it has engendered and engenders still!" Or they might go on to say, "You must admit that this last week you have been singing,

> 'Beneath the cross of Jesus
> I fain would take my stand.'

The symbol of Christianity is a tragedy. When you call yourselves most Christian you stand in the shadow of a Cross. Your very churches are built cruciform. You describe duty as bearing a cross. Christianity does not make people happy. Shall we leave all the gayety and delight, the transient pleasures which yet are sweet, to stand in the shadow of a Cross and expect to be happy?" You know how many people there are who take such an attitude.

Moreover, there is some truth in it. Christianity does sober life. As a friend of mine said, Paul might have died with his head in a bed instead of on a block if he had not been a Christian. David Livingstone might have died in peace in a Scotch home instead of in the heart of Africa if he had not been a Christian. Real Christianity does make life serious and sacrificial. It takes young women who might live in luxury at home and puts them into settlement houses in the slums of our great cities. It takes a young missionary like Henry Martyn, graduating from the university with the ball at his feet so far as worldly success is concerned, and sends him to India to burn out for God. Some of *us* might have lived easier lives if

Christ had not touched our consciences, if we had not really cared about people and the future of mankind. Christianity does make life serious.

That is why this attack which Freud and other psychologists are making on religion, and which is bothering some of you, is so largely false. They say that religion is wish-fulfillment, that religious people run away from the stern facts of life and seek retreat in an imaginary world of peace and love, God, and immortality. They say that men, wanting to be happy and discovering that they cannot be happy with the stern realities of life, make up a fantasy world of their own, a comfortable, religious refuge to which they can retreat to find happiness, so that being religious is like reading detective stories: it is running away from actual facts to fantasy and coming back somewhat rested from your mental holiday.

Undoubtedly there is a great deal of that kind of religion, and more than once in this pulpit you have heard the dangers of it pointed out. But does one mean to say that when Christ tackled that problem in Jerusalem—the degeneracy of its religious leaders, the inhumanity of its attitude toward the outcast, the greed of its temple ring—when he made up his mind that he would clean up the situation or die, until, uncompromising and unafraid, he bore his Cross out toward Golgotha, he was merely trying to be happy and escape from the stern realities of life into a comfortable world of religious fantasy? Does one mean to say that when David Livingstone went out to Africa

75

to wrestle with one of the most forbidding facts of his generation—the slave trade of the dark continent—that when he left his wife's body buried under a great tree on the coast and wrote in his diary, "Oh my Mary, my Mary! how often we have longed for a quiet home, since you and I were cast adrift at Kolobeng," and then turned his face toward the last terrific journey into the interior—all that was like reading detective stories to escape from the stern facts of life into comfortable religious fantasy?

No, real Christianity is not within a thousand miles of this thing that Freud is shooting at. Read the stories of the great Christians, of Paul beheaded on the Appian Road, of Augustine standing like a tower of brass unshaken in his episcopal city of Hippo in North Africa while the barbarians were hammering at the city gates—a long catalog of those fearless men who grappled with the dark and dirty facts of life and in extremities were of excellent hope. They were not retreating into fairy land. Christianity at its best has set men to facing life's real facts, has given them faith, courage, and radiance to meet them, has made men serious and sacrificial. But, strangely enough, that is why it has made them radiantly happy so that out of the heart of the best living in Christendom, as in the New Testament, there comes that cry, "This is life eternal."

The pathos of the situation is that of all the millions of people who are trying so hard to be happy, one knows that only a few of them will succeed. Do you remember what the dope fiends have named their dope—"happiness dust"? That is a significant name —"happiness dust." There are other forms of "happiness dust" beside dope. See the millions of addicts to their diverse forms of "happiness dust"! They all keep increasing the dose.

To change the figure, when they find that they are missing happiness they speed up their pace. Woodrow Wilson defined a fanatic as a man who misses his aim and then redoubles his energy. Multitudes of people all around us are seeking for happiness like that until, satiated but not satisfied (what a difference there is between the meaning of those two words from the same stem!), they sink down little by little to the common levels of modern disillusionment and cynicism: "Man hath no preëminence above a beast: for all is foolishness."

If this is the truth, let us come to personal grips with it. What is it that puts meaning into life? What is it that can reproduce in our experience that cry of the New Testament, "This is life eternal"?

Faith in something—always that. Nobody ever yet said, "This is life eternal," who did not find something in which he could honestly put his faith.

Those who call us modernists and dislike us accordingly, are constantly accusing us of trying to break down the people's faith. That is a strange accusation. The fact is that all around us we see people losing faith. That is the trouble. Their faith has been associated by artificial adhesion with things that they can no longer think tenable, and in consequence they go out into this generation trying to live without anything to put their faith in, until they end by debunking everything that is excellent and of a good report, and crying, "All is foolishness!" And what we, who constructively are interested in liberal Christianity, are driving at is to give people a faith they will not have to lose. After all, it is faith in something that makes life worth living.

Henry Van Dyke said of this age that "its coat-of-arms is an interrogation point rampant, above three bishops dormant, and its motto is *Query?*" Now, some of us have found something we do positively believe in. God, for example. "This is life eternal, to know thee the only true God." The alternative is plain enough.

> The world rolls round for ever like a mill;
> It grinds out death and life and good and ill;
> It has no purpose, heart or mind or will.

That is to say, ultimately all is foolishness.

Of course, there are great questions about God. How could it be otherwise? The idea of God is the most august conception that man's imagination ever tried to deal with. Of course there are unanswered problems. God is like the ocean—vast—wide areas of it cold, forbidding, but through it a gulf stream that is warm and fructifying. There are wide areas of His operation in the universe that I cannot understand, but there is a spiritual gulf stream there that

78

evidences itself in man and his spiritual progress. It reveals itself in the Christlike possibilities of human nature. That cannot be an accident.

God is in all that liberates and lifts.

I believe in God, and in man as the son of God with capacities to become superman and then again superman, rising on stepping stones of his dead self to higher things, with hopes that death cannot stop. For any man who gains even that much honest faith in God and man, life has stopped being meaningless. It is getting meaning now.

Faith in something, devotion to something—always that. If ever anybody says, "This is life eternal!" he has found something greater than himself to which he has given himself.

Contrast a brush pile with a tree. What is the difference? Look at them—made of the same material, with the same chemical composition and the same wooden fabric. But the difference is immense. A tree is organized and a brush pile is not. A tree is integrated, unified, and alive, and a brush heap is only one detail piled on another. That is the difference between lives. There are many men who would give almost anything to be able to say, "This is life!" and they have tried to get it by piling one detail on another. They accumulate things, thrills, sensations. When they find they are missing happiness they speed up their pace and pile more details on more details until they get a brush heap of existence, very big, but miss the whole secret of life, which is something else: organizing oneself around devotions to which one gives oneself. Do not be a brush pile. Be a tree.

My friends, the debunkers of all the common decencies and moralities of life have had their innings about long enough. It is high time somebody began debunking the debunkers, and in particular how much one would like to substitute for that silly slogan, Let yourself go! that indispensable slogan, Pull yourself together! Let yourself go! disperses life into its details. Pull yourself together! organizes life into its unities. When we were very little boys and we let ourselves go in bad temper, a paternal voice would say to us, Young man, you pull yourself together! When we were in the trenches and, as the men said, were "getting our wind up" over some difficulty or danger, some voice, perhaps with expletives not quotable here, would say, You men, pull yourselves together! That word is indispensable for any real living.

Those first disciples heard it. They, too, were aimless. They too had not found out yet what their life meant, and then Christ came and you can see them pulling themselves together around him and his cause. That is also in our text. There is purposefulness there. "This is life eternal, that they might know thee the only true God, and Jesus Christ, whom thou hast sent."

Faith in something, devotion to something, hope for something—always that. Anybody who ever said,

"This is life eternal!" had hope. One could not leave that accent out on Easter morning. Death is not the end. I honestly and thoughtfully believe that. Do you? I have as many unanswered questions as anybody here about the details that lie after death but I am confident that life lies after death. It did with Jesus. I have as many unanswered questions as anybody here about the physical details of those resurrection stories, but that is not the gist of the matter. He could not be holden by death. Death had no dominion over him. He is not dead. He is alive. I believe in immortality. But what I am concerned about for myself and for you is not immortality but life eternal. To have a quality of experience so rich and radiant, so full of meaning that it makes going on worth while —may God bestow on us that Easter gift!

Prayer

Eternal God, our Father, we beseech Thee that Thy grace may penetrate to the inner life of some one here. Cross Thou the thresholds where we have forbidden Thee. Open Thou the doors that we have locked against Thee. Shine through the windows that we have shuttered. And let us, who have come up to a festival, go down facing our consciences. O God, Who hast surrounded us with such infinite privilege for richness and radiance of life, forgive us for our spiritual poverty. Lead us into life eternal for Christ's sake. Amen.

Belief in Immortality as a Spiritual Achievement

LYNN HAROLD HOUGH,
D.D., Litt.D., LL.D.

Lynn Harold Hough was born in Cadiz, Ohio, September 10th, 1877, and graduated from Scio College in Ohio, his further educational work having been taken in Drew Theological Seminary, with Post Graduate work in New York University.

He taught church history in Garratt Biblical School, and was for a year the President of Northwestern University in Evanston, Ill. While he remained the chief executive of this university for only a year he set in motion the machinery which looked forward to the lake front campus in Chicago which was probably the greatest forward move this school has had in all of its history.

Called from the presidency of Northwestern University to Central Methodist Church in Detroit, Michigan in 1920 he only recently left this great pulpit to accept the pastorate of the American Presbyterian Church in Montreal, Canada.

He is the author of a full Book Shelf of his own, numbering some twenty-five volumes, including the product of several outstanding college lectureships which he has been chosen to give from time to time. He is one of the most popular preachers to college students in America, and is an authority on church history, and on the life and works of Dante and Browning. He is one of the few speakers who is invited year after year to speak before the most famous of all the Browning Societies that one in Boston, Mass. He is a popular preacher in England and for several Summers has supplied the pulpits of the City Temple in London and Carrs Lane in Birmingham, England.

He has been prominent in Masonic work and belongs to many clubs of a social and literary nature.

Belief in Immortality as a Spiritual Achievement

By Lynn Harold Hough, Pastor American Presbyterian Church, Montreal, Canada

"Our inward man is renewed day by day."
—II COR. IV: 16

"There," said the cynic as he looked at the saint, "is a man who believes." The spectacle of a great believer is a quickening experience. The man who has organized his life about a few high beliefs is an inspiring person. The man to whom the belief in immortality is not a difficult problem but has become a glowing assurance has all sorts of secrets of effective activity shining in his eyes. The man of great beliefs is the man of great achievements.

You can test a civilization by its capacity for tremendous beliefs. The civilization which has become unable to believe in immortality has ceased to deserve immortality. If an age cherishes values which deserve to sweep triumphantly past the menace of death that age is sure to believe in immortality.

You can paint a picture of human life which makes belief in immortality seem the veriest impertinence. And certain aspects of human experience go far to justify the picture. That master of swift and deadly

85

irony, the second century Syrian Lucian who wrote so potently in Greek, was the author of an astonishing little dialogue entitled "Charon."

The ferryman of the underworld has gotten leave from Pluto to take a day off and has come up to see the world which mortals feel so sad at leaving. Hermes with the help of Charon piles a few mountains one upon the other and so they have a fairly wide view of the world which men leave for the place of the dead. Then Hermes arranges for a more intimate view and they look upon human folly and futility and vain ambition together. They look at Milo of Croton the athlete. He is mightily elated because he has just picked up a bull and carried it along the race course amid the applause of the Greeks. "Does it occur to him that he must die some day?" asks Charon. They look at powerful monarchs who are to come upon days of doom, and some of whom are to die violent or shameful deaths. Charon, the ferryman of the underworld, is vastly amused. Then they look at "the common herd." Charon sums these up in a couple of biting sentences. "Their cities remind me of beehives. Every man keeps a sting for his neighbor's service; and a few like wasps make spoil of their weaker brethren." The air around them is full of misty shapes—hopes, fears, follies, shames, greeds, hates, grudges, and the like. "My dear Charon," says Hermes, "there is no word for the absurdity of it. They do take it all so seriously, that is the best of it; and then, long before they have finished their schem-

86

ing, up comes good old Death, and whisks them off, and all is over. . . . There are a few who see through the vanity of it all, but they merely stand aloof from the rest of mankind, and scoff at all that goes on." There is fatal folly and there is cold and terrible cynicism and that is all.

Now it is clear that if there is no more to say, immortality itself would be a rather sorry jest. One does not see quite why these lives so empty of deep and noble meaning should be prolonged. The real tragedy is not death. It is the sort of living which death brings to an end.

But this is not the whole story. There was a great deal going on in the world which Charon and Hermes seem to have missed that day. Of course one remembers that Lucian gave their eyes to Charon and Hermes. And Lucian was always stronger in caustic criticism than in hearty appreciation. All about the world, good was fighting with evil, love was coming into contact with hate. There were mothers who forgot themselves in the prosperity of their children. There were friends who put loyalty above life. And the deep spiritual realities were saliently active among the children of men. That day above the old Mediterranean world Charon and Hermes had eyes for everything except the redeeming virtues which give hope to the life of man.

The most significant fact about human life is just the emergence of values which give to the world a new meaning and in whose presence death is seen for the deceiver that he is. As the inward man begins to be renewed day by day you confront a new situation whose meaning cannot be interpreted in terms of mortality.

Clearly the experience does not have to do with things which can be handled. Yet something subtly potent does manage to enter into human life. Emily Dickinson was thinking of such an experience when she wrote:

> He ate and drank the precious words,
> His spirit grew robust;
> He knew no more that he was poor,
> Nor that his frame was dust.
> He danced along the dingy days,
> And this bequest of wings
> Was but a book. What liberty
> A loosened spirit brings.[1]

So much for assertion. Now let us put our assertion into the form of a question: What values have emerged in human life which have in them the seed of immortality?

First there is the sense of truth as something to which you must be loyal at any cost. The moment you begin to think of truth as something which has a right to demand your allegiance, something superior to physical pleasure or pain and transcending physical comfort, you have already passed out of the world of mortality and entered into the world of eternal values. To suffer for the truth is already to reach a region

[1] Used by permission of Little, Brown & Co., publishers of *The Poems of Emily Dickinson*.

beyond the clanging gates which physical death swings shut.

Then there is beauty as something greater than any particular expression of beauty. You thrill in the presence of the gold edged with purple which is a particular sunset. But at last there comes to you a sense of that beauty which lies back of all the sunsets which have been and of all the sunsets which will be. For a moment the physical is shot through with golden loveliness. That is tonight's sunset. But there is a beauty which shines in every lovely thing and yet is beyond them all, a beauty which gives a soul of loveliness to the material world. As you give yourself to the thought of this beauty, as you try to express it in lovely words, or to capture it in the net of mind, or to pour it out in the graciousness of daily living, you have already passed into a realm which mortality cannot touch. Your life is already renewed by deathless beauty even in the midst of a world of decay.

Whenever you meet goodness you confront another challenge to mortality. It was a fine tribute which was paid to the Bishop of London. " 'Look at 'em! Just look at 'em!' said the bus driver, training his whip toward the crowd gathered round the bishop, preaching from the open air pulpit at St. James, Piccadilly. 'There's something 'uman about 'im, I've 'eard 'im down East many a time, and I tell you, when you 'ave been a-listening to 'im for a bit, a kind of clean feeling takes 'old on you, same's if it was your day off, and

you'd 'ad a bath and got your Sunday suit on.' "[1] That
something out of the very character of the Bishop of
London which got into his words and moved men, was
something we have all met at one time or another. And
goodness always does put our minds into a region
where it is always easier for us to believe all sorts of
splendid things. Goodness transcends the material
order. It is a value which belongs to eternity. And
at once it makes immortality a new sort of belief. It
now comes to be the belief that goodness cannot die.
And the belief is all the easier because we have a
curious feeling that you cannot exhaust goodness. So
it has the seed of immortality in it. Not merely does
it deserve eternal life. It is in quality itself eternal.

The experience of deep and genuine human fellowship often transcends the limitations which belong to
mortality. To love men as Professor Rauschenbusch
loved them is to enter a region where the biology of
time becomes incidental. You can only love men
with the greatest sort of love by assuming that they
have a kind of infinite worth. You must lift them
into the region of permanent values before you can
give to them the greatest devotion. The great friends
of men have been those who considered mankind to
possess a value beyond price. Great saints like Francis
de Sales were always seeing in men more than men
saw in themselves. "Be worth saving," cried Emman-
uel Bayard to the drunken sailor whom he had saved
from drowning, and who suddenly sobered and looked

[1] *Prophets, Priests and Kings,* by A. G. Gardiner, p. 167.

with bewilderment at the powerful and magnificent young man who had rescued him, muttering that he was not worth such risks as Bayard had taken. The fiery confidence back of that phrase, "Be worth saving," has a noble world of beautiful fellowship in it. "Feed my lambs," said Jesus to the friend who had deceived him. The very offer of such fellowship takes us out of time and puts us into eternity. Death has no dominion in the world of moral fellowship. You have here a kind of value which death cannot touch.

And multitudes of men have gone further. They have found satisfaction in what they confidently declared to be fellowship with the living God. Jesus seized upon this in his imperial way. God is not the God of the dead but of the living, he declared. To know God is to share the triumphant life of God. Such was the faith of Jesus. Such was the confidence he bequeathed to the world. The Old Testament saint was sure of God even before he began to think of immortality. But at last he saw as some of the greatest of the Psalms make clear enough that to have such a God as a friend was to be transported to a realm where death simply could not have the final word. And the men of the New Testament quite simply came to realize that their fellowship with Christ took quite away the sting of death, and the power of the grave. All sepulchers are open sepulchers to those who know the meaning of that high fellowship.

Of one more value which transcends the limits of mortality we must say a word. This value is Sacrifice.

"Nobody denies," wrote Dr. Horace J. Bridges, "that gallant gentlemen, whose talents and genius the world could ill spare, did a splendidly right thing, when in the wreck of the Titanic, they stood aside and accepted certain death to give a chance for life to stewardesses and immigrant women." We are fairly abashed by the moral magnificence of such actions. And whatever else they may mean, they surely do mean that here you touch values in whose presence death is without power. Such attitudes challenge eternity to justify them. Great self-sacrifice sets a standard to which the vast scheme of things simply must measure up.

All these far-flung values—the greatness of truth, the imperishable quality of beauty, the vistas of goodness, the abiding satisfaction of fellowship, human and divine, the strange wonder of sacrifice, are things we reach by taking adventures in their name. When we take risks for them they become our own possession. And if we take risks in the name of all of them we find that the inward man is renewed by a force which has its own vast power. To fight for these things and to make them our own is to come into a new world. And as we dwell in that world we discover that immortality has ceased to be a problem. It has become an authentic and undeniable experience.

The Easter Doubt

EDWIN HOLT HUGHES,
D.D., Litt.D., LL.D.

Edwin Holt Hughes is in the center
of three generations of Methodist
ministers, his father having been a famous Methodist minister, and his son,
Edwin Holt Hughes, of the present
generation, being also in the Methodist ministry, with a brother, Matthew
Simpson Hughes, deceased, also a
Bishop in the Methodist Episcopal
Church.

Bishop Hughes was born in
Moundsville, West Virginia, Dec.
7th, 1866, and attended college at
West Virginia State University and
Ohio Wesleyan University, from
which he graduated in 1889; receiving
the degree of D.D. from the same
school in 1892 and an LL.D. in 1909.
He graduated from Boston University
School of Theology in 1892 and
served for a few years as pastor of
Methodist churches in Newton Center
and Malden, Mass. from whence he
was called to the Presidency of De-
Pauw University at thirty-seven years
of age, he then being the youngest
President of a major university in the
United States. In 1908 he was elected
a Bishop in the Methodist Episcopal
Church at the age of forty-two.

He has served as Bishop in the

San Francisco Area, at which time he was Chairman of all religious activities at the Panama Pacific International Exposition. His next task was that of Bishop of the Boston Area, at which time he was Acting President of Boston University for a year, and now he is the Bishop of the Chicago Area. He has always been a leader in educational matters in the church world, and is the author of several books of sermons. He is known primarily, however, as a great preacher and it is an honor to present his sermon in this series.

The Easter Doubt

By EDWIN HOLT HUGHES, CHICAGO, ILL.

"They yet believed not for joy."
—LUKE XXIV: 41

HERE is the cause of this message! Years ago I
concluded that many persons were failing to believe in our holy faith because it was so very wonderful in its promise. The phrase "too good to be true"
kept sounding in my heart, even as I had often heard
it uttered by others. I concluded to preach a sermon
about it all. I waited long for a proper text that
surely held the idea. Then one day these words flashed
out of the holy page, and the following message came.

It is significant that a man can be blinded by light
even as by darkness. The darkness that struck Paul
on the Damascus road, when the excess of radiance fell
on his eyes, was as dense as any that had blinded him
at any previous midnight. And there is a pain that
arises from happiness as well as from sadness. There
is a grip that one feels at the throat, a pressure that
one feels at the heart, when one comes home from afar
as well as when one departs. Sometimes one mood
borrows the expression of its opposite; we tremble for
gladness; we weep for joy. It is as if we became con-

95

fused in the deeper and more sacred moments, lost ourselves in a medley of feelings, and used the evidence of faith for the arousing of disbelief.

We all know that there is a doubt that arises from despair. Something has happened within our experience that led us to say: "It is too terrible! We cannot believe it!" Often indeed, after some great sorrow has fallen upon us, we feel as if the loved one gone must cross the threshold, as if the familiar voice must once more greet us. Each morning we have anew the doubt that arises from our grim sorrow. We awake to the light of the day only to live through the dreadful ordeal once more, only to compel ourselves into the awful realization. This is the doubt that grows out of pain. There are some things that we are slow to believe because of our sadness.

There is also a doubt that springs from joy. When we come up out of the burning delirium of fever and know that our life has been spared, we tend to doubt the reality of our health. When we emerge from the financial crisis and stand again in the midst of good fortune, we doubt the assurance of our success. When we see a dear one come back to us from the borders of the other country, the color flushing the cheek that had been so wan, the sprightliness dashing the manner that had been so subdued; when we hear the physician saying: "The worst is over, and all will be well now"— we doubt the reality of the unbroken home. Our joy cancels our faith. We say: "It is too good to be true!" How often we have heard that statement! It means that there are some experiences wherein we believe not "for joy," hours when the very skepticism of happiness takes hold on us and the glory of life leads us into a region of gloom.

Thus do we stand between our hesitation to accept the things that are fear-inspiring and our hesitation to accept the things that are joy-inspiring. This same spirit works in the religious realm. We are often skeptical about the tragic and glorious truths of the Christian faith. We believe not its warnings because they are too terrible. We believe not its promises because they are too gracious. We banish hell because it is so unspeakably awful; we banish heaven because it is so unspeakably grand. Unless we are careful, we come at last to accept only the small and commonplace beliefs. We fail to take warning from the fearful things; we fail to gain inspiration from the precious things. So life may become mediocre; for every man must see large losses to shun and large gains to seek ere his motives move on large planes.

Nor is this strange law of doubt one that applies only to the religious life. Its preeminent field may be there, but not its sole field. Religion deals with the unseen—an unseen God, an unseen hell, an unseen heaven. But, whenever we think of the thing that is hidden from our experience in any way, doubt is apt to arise. Apart from our actual vision there are many facts that we would find it hard to believe. If we had never seen fish, it would be incredible to our thought that life could sustain itself by breathing water. If we had

97

never seen birds, it would be incredible that anything could carry itself in mid-air and use parts of its own body as propellers. If we had never seen flowers, it would be incredible that a dead-appearing seed could pierce the hard earth by its rootlets, and the air with its fingers, and so could fashion itself into surpassing vesture. The Easter lily, like the resurrection whose truth it symbolizes, is itself a miracle. It is only because some wonders fall within our constant experience that we credit them. Prior to our actual contact with them, what we call the Easter doubt would work its way into our minds and we would believe not for very wonder.

That skepticism follows us into quite another region. Our wonder may defeat our faith prior to our experience of the work of God in his natural world. But the same thing may be said about the accomplishments of men under the leadership of the divine providence. Prophecy as to what man may do in the future is apt to be heavily discounted. In the past it would surely have been doubted because of the wonder of the listeners. Suppose that you had stood two hundred years ago in the presence of men and had told them of the achievements of the next two centuries. You would have said: "Instead of yonder sailboat which crosses the ocean after a voyage of weary months, a boat veered by every wind and whipped by every tempest, there will be a vast ship, propelled by the steam that pours from yonder kettle—a boat that will take you over the waters in five days." They would have replied: "That fairytale is too good to believe. You are a dreamer." Suppose that you had said: "Instead of that stage which takes the whole day to run from Plymouth to Boston, we shall some day have steam cars that will carry the people back or to within an hour," they would still have doubted the prophecy on account of its beneficence. The story of the telegraph line, or the cable line, or the telephone, or the radio, or the moving picture, would have excited only laughter. Men would have answered your enthusiasm by saying: "All of these things would be monumental; but we shall not have them; such promises are too good to come true." All progress, prior to experience, is to the most of us incredible. If some man endued with prophetic power were to detail the changes in transportation and communication that are sure to take place in the future—no one of us would credit the good news. Should these changes be predicted as coming within our lifetime, we should know, in a lower way, the meaning of the Easter doubt and should not believe for joy.

In religion the doubt arising from joy plays its largest havoc. For here we deal with the unseen and eternal. The more thrilling any spiritual truth is, the more will our poor distrustful natures be prone to call it into question, even though it be likewise true that we still cling to it as too precious to be wholly surrendered. This quality of doubt especially attaches to the truth of Easter Day. We need not wonder if we have been affected by it; for the early disciples were its victims. When the risen Christ appeared to them and gave the evidence of his resurrection by showing them his hands and feet, it is written: "They yet believed not for joy." They were merely saying within themselves: "It is too good to be true." They did not quite analyze their own feelings; but they were actually doubting because of the radiant and comforting meaning of his presence. Unless we are careful the type of skepticism that met that first Easter revelation will put all the grand essentials of our faith under its peculiar blight.

Consider, first, the foundation idea—our faith in a good God. The most of us do not appreciate the meanings given to life by that great creed. We say: "I believe in God the Father Almighty." What a wonderful faith it is! Over us is One of omnipotent power, of unerring wisdom, of unfailing goodness! One who marks the falling of the sparrows and counts the hairs of the heads of His children! One who keeps an eternal and sleepless vigil above the subjects of His kingdom! What can be greater and more inspiring than to have such a God! We need to be careful lest we turn from this revelation because it is so good! In our best moments that faith takes hold of us supremely; our hearts are held by a subdued gladness; we actually lean upon the arms of the Lord. Then, almost ere we recognize the strange process, our joy leads on to doubt. We begin to question because of our very happiness. We, too, believe not for joy. We need to remind ourselves forcibly that the goodness and greatness of a truth constitute in themselves no reason for its rejection. The world cannot live without the sun. All growth would cease; all light fail; all warmth vanish; all life die. But the value and beauty of the sun offer no reason for denying its power. We should be careful not to blot out God from the heaven of life merely because He is so great, so wise, so loving. In spite of questioning joy He is still God over all, blessed forevermore!

Much the same thing may be said about Jesus Christ. If there be this gracious God, can you think of anything that you would rather have Him do than to come out of the world of spirit and show Himself to His children? The heart of man has been ever saying: "Shew us the Father, and it sufficeth us." Could God better teach us how to live than to live on earth Himself? Could he better make us ashamed of our sins and woo our love than by dying for us? But is there not, likewise, a tendency to doubt the incarnation with its wonderful inspirations for life just simply because the record is "too good to be true"? Is there not a danger that our joy shall defeat our trust? Are we always able to overcome the foolish doubt that arises from the preciousness of revelation? Do we find it possible to stand in the presence of the incarnate God and still hold fast both to our ecstasy and to our faith?

This brings us forward to the special lesson as it relates to immortality. Christ came; that was much. Christ lived a spotless life on earth; that was more. Christ died on the cross for us; that was still more. And yet how incomplete the record would have been if that had been the end! In a certain sense it is the empty tomb that makes a full faith. So we see the form laid in the sepulchre, amid the last kindly offices of the burial spices. The brightest being that our world has seen has died a death of disgrace. No wonder that the disciples went sadly back to their old occupations. A little while later, drawn together by the tie of his discipleship, they are in a room. It is the evening of the first Easter day. Suddenly, without the opening of a door or a window, One stands before them. Their hearts are bursting with awful surprise. They hear the same old accents: "Peace be unto you!" They see pierced hands extended for their credence. They behold him as he persuades them into the faith of the resurrection. Still it is written: "They yet believed not for joy." This assurance is what their souls demand; it gratifies all their holier longings. But they actually doubt it because it is so good!

Why did not Thomas believe in the resurrection? Was it not because it seemed too good to be true? Should we not be heedful lest we fall into the doubt that grows out of joy? It may be that often we shall meet the risen Lord and fail to trust—because of the beauty and cheer of the Easter revelation. We may well guard ourselves against that recklessness of doubt that rejects a truth simply because the truth fills us with holy gladness.

When we run the Easter truth out into its conclusion for us, we may still be followed by the same form of skepticism. We repeat the glorious words: "If we believe that Jesus rose from the dead, them also that sleep in Jesus will God bring with him." You may remember the legend of the insects that lived in the muddy pool. There came to them a "revelation from above," as they felt strange stirrings of prophecy within themselves, that some day they would be lifted out of their abode, would be given wings, and would fly from flower to flower in a strange medium called the air. The word seemed wonderful. So they agreed that, if that glorious change should come, those that were promoted would come back to assure the rest of the awaiting glory. The change did come to some of them. They flew in the azure; they passed from blossom to blossom; they floated in the sunlight. They wanted to give their message to the companions of the old life; but they flew over the surface of the pool and found that the conditions of the new life were so different from those of the old, that each must wait to experience the glad change for himself! The legend is true to our lives. We are shut up in this lower realm. We feel strange stirrings within us. We have received the word that some day we shall go out into a higher sphere, filled with endless beauty and joy. We, too, may be staggered by the greatness of this revelation. Our very joy may lead us into doubt. Those we love have gone away; our mothers, our fathers, our children, our friends have one by one slipped away from our side, and we see and hear them no more. Shall we meet them again? O Christ of Easter, dost thou say "Yes"? Is this the message for our broken homes? Oh, the glory of the revelation! What thrilling joy is this that lays strong hold upon us? Then the Easter doubt works its way into our hopeful mood. We say to ourselves: "My heart yearns for this truth; I see the delight of the promise; I long to see again my mother, my father, my little child, my old dear friend. But it seems too good to be true." Is it not a transcript of the disciples' experience recorded in the words: "They yet believed not for joy"? Let us not allow our gladness to deceive us into doubt. Let us follow Christ beyond the tomb; let us see him standing on the other side of death; let us hear his words with ceaseless faith: "I am he that liveth, and was dead; and, behold, I am alive for evermore, . . . and have the keys of hell and of death." Let us rise up to these great truths; let us live by them and in them and for them. Then shall the Easter Doubt be defeated by the Easter Faith and all our lives shall take on the radiant hope of the Festival of Immortality.

The Image of Immortality

JOHN A. HUTTON, D.D., Litt.D., LL.D.

John A. Hutton, for many years a famous Scotch minister, is now the Editor of the widely read *British Weekly*.

He has been a popular Summer preacher at assemblies and gatherings of church people in the United States for several years. He is especially popular at our American Chautauqua gatherings.

The author of several books, the first one to become a best seller in the religious field was *Guidance in Matters of Faith from Robert Browning* and this book went through many editions. He is a specialist in the field of the Russian writers of the last half century and is also well informed and writes most fascinatingly in the field of the English poets, his particular hobby being Browning.

Many of his books of sermons find large audiences not only in England where they are first published but in the United States, where Dr. Hutton has a vast following of friends.

Since becoming editor of the influential British weekly he has not had so much time for traveling and speaking in the United States but from time to time we still get his viewpoints in such sermons and books as this one. No book of this description would be quite complete unless it had a sermon by Dr. Hutton in it, as a representative of one of the first dozen great preachers of Great Britain.

The Image of Immortality

By John A. Hutton, Editor of "The British Weekly," London

"The Eternal God is thy refuge, and underneath are the everlasting arms."

—DEUT. XXXIII: 27

T HE belief in immortality is a belief not peculiar to Christianity. In fact "I believe in the immortality of the soul" is not essentially a Christian pronouncement at all. The Christian pronouncement which takes the place of a parallel pronouncement in various religious systems is something more concrete and decisive. As we have it in the Apostles' Creed, the Christian affirmation is "I believe in the resurrection of the body." That is to say, from the beginning, those who had learned from Christ had the daring to believe that, after the apparent triumph of death over us all, it was no mere vague and intangible essence which survived; it was the human being, the total personality, the recognizable man or woman, who passed on and encountered God!

I

Firm and unyielding as is the Christian proposition, it has never been denied that to hold such a confidence is a matter of Faith. It rests finally not upon argument. There is a sense in which, if you like to say so, belief in the resurrection of the dead "begs the question." If you like, you may say that in all reasonings upon ultimate matters there is a "pathetic fallacy." Christianity concedes all these things when it introduces its affirmation by the words "I believe."

Now on all sides I hold that it would be an immense clearing of the air were we to make this perfectly plain at the outset: *There is no coercive proof for the objective reality of anything that you and I believe.* If there were such an objective and coercive proof, what would result, so far as we are concerned, would be not faith but *sight;* and we live not by sight but by faith. As Pascal put the case: "The heart has its own reasons which the reason does not know." But that is another way of saying that the insights, the pressures here and there, the lights and shadows, of which the soul of man may be aware, all take place in a region *not contrary to reason*, but earlier than the intellectual faculty, and in the great issues of life and death more peremptory and decisive.

II

When Christians have been challenged on this high belief of theirs, they have, in the days of their highest wisdom, refused to haggle over the evidence this way or that. What then have they done? *They have simply fallen back upon the character of God.* They have taken their stand here—that, if God be thus and thus, certain things are morally inevitable; because the absence of such things would be the denial of His being, or of His sovereignty. And so, when driven into the last ditch, not merely by reasons which men in cold blood could bring forward, but by the apparent contradictions in their own human experience, great believers in God like Job have been content to fall back upon Him, and to say, "Though he slay me, yet will I trust in him!"

All this is not for one moment to concede that life itself, and that the documents of the Christian Faith, provide no *corroborations* of the great belief which, we declare again, rests finally upon the character of God. But those corroborations which life and the documents of our Faith provide are themselves not coercively decisive unless for those who have already, under the disciples of God, come upon *a tenderness of the spirit* which has given them the hearing ear and the seeing eye for the finer hints of truth.

III

The romantic literature of the nineteenth century which arose in a mighty protest against the insinuations, as they seemed at that time, of scientific categories, rallied at once, and by a sure instinct dug itself in, on this impregnable position. Arthur Hugh Clough wrote and sang

If hopes were dupes, fears may be liars beyond.

Tennyson everywhere! For example here:

> Thou wilt not leave us in the dust!
> Thou madest man, he knows not why;
> He thinks he was not made to die;
> And Thou hast made him: Thou art just!

Robert Browning in a thousand passages; but take this:

> When I see day succeed the deepest night
> How can I speak but as I know?—My speech
> Must be, throughout the darkness, "It will end:
> The light that did burn will burn."
> So never I lose footing in the maze
> No! I have light nor fear the dark at all!

Or again:

> For sudden the worst turns the best to the brave,
> The black minute's at end,
> And the elements' rage, the fiend voices that rave,
> Shall dwindle, shall blend,
> Shall change, shall become first a piece out of pain,
> Then a light, then thy breast
> Oh thou soul of my soul, I shall clasp at length
> And with God be at rest!

And so one might go on ranging great literature through all races, and through all times, in defence of the unconquerable confidence of man, rooted in something which he felt was of the very essence of his being, that "a cosmos" (to quote Lotze) "cannot have chaos for its crown!"

THE IMAGE OF IMMORTALITY

IV

Now finally, and most astonishingly, you will find, in my own view, the best and most vigorous and most simple statement of all these things in a quite obscure, and most unlikely place in the Bible—away back, in fact, in the Book of Judges!

The words which I am going to quote, as embodying in simple naïve language, the irreducible and inexpugnable persuasion of the religious soul, were spoken by a woman who, I believe, had not any notion of what a sublime thing she had said!

And yet, I declare, she said something which anticipated the whole of Dante, and the entire output of the Romantic literature of the western world! She forestalled Browning and Tennyson, and had already said what every radiant spirit in its rapturous and creative days has ever tried to say!

The woman I mean, was the mother of Samson! The story all Biblical students already know.

Her husband Manoah rushed into her presence one day, as many a man has rushed into the presence of his wife since, in a panic. He doubtless had at the moment the face of a man who is at the end of his resources! I take it upon me, therefore, to suggest that his wife said, "What is the matter now?" And he replied in effect, "Oh, it is too terrible even to begin to tell you!" But at last he was persuaded to become articulate. And this is what he said: "We shall surely die, because we have seen God!" What did he mean?

Oh, he meant just this. Something wonderful had happened to him. He had seen what he thought was an angel. And please do not allow any of us, in these so clever and superficial days of ours, to conclude that, because we do not see angels, Manoah did not see angels: that indeed he did not see anything!

The fact is that a man called Manoah said that he saw something which he declared was God. It was so good and so wonderful and so overwhelming! Taking too literally a belief of his own people, he supposed that, having had this tremendous experience, he should forthwith die! He had rushed, therefore, into the presence of his wife, and he had said, "We shall surely die, because we have seen God."

Now it was there and then that that wife of his said something so deep, and so final, that there is nothing more to be said for ever along that line! Not only did she anticipate the Dantes, and the Tennysons, and the Brownings; she anticipated all the Gifford lecturers, and all the Bampton, and all the Hibbert lecturers, who have ever lectured, or who will ever lecture! What did she say then? She said, simply speaking out of her own unsophisticated heart, "If the Lord were pleased to kill us, he would not have received a burnt offering and a meat offering, at our hands, *neither would he have shewed us all these things*, or would as at this time have told us such things as these!"

That I hold is an insight beyond which and deeper than which there is nothing to be said by the lips of man. It is a falling back upon the justice of God! It is as though that simple woman had said to her frightened husband, "Is *that* what you think of God? Do you think we are in the hands of a Being who lifts us up in order to fling us down? Who teases us with things beyond ourselves, so that He may mock at our pathetic ambitions? If the Lord had been pleased to slay us, it would have been sheer malice for Him to call us on, as He has done, only that He might thwart us, and humiliate us at the end! And more than that. He took a gift from us! He shared a meal with us! What would you think of someone, of anyone, who had entered our narrow little home, who had shared something with us, who had even taken something from us, and who there and then could plan our destruction, or look on while we were being destroyed?"

"Nay, that be far from Thee, Oh God! Shall not the Judge of all the earth be right!"

Therefore to whom turn I but to Thee, the ineffable Name?
Builder and maker Thou, of houses not made with hands!
What, have fear of change from Thee who art ever the same?
Doubt that Thy power can fill the heart that Thy power
    expands?
There shall never be one lost good! What was shall live as
    before.
The evil is null, is nought, is silence implying sound,
What was good shall be good, with, for evil, so much good
    more;
On the earth the broken arcs, in the Heaven the perfect round.

The God of the Living

CHARLES EDWARD JEFFERSON, D.D., LL.D.

Charles E. Jefferson was born in Cambridge, Ohio, August 29th, 1860, graduated from Ohio Wesleyan University in 1882, taught school for a short time and enrolled in Boston University School of Theology graduating in 1887.

He was ordained into the Congregational Ministry in 1887, the same year he was married, and has only served two churches, one at Chelsea, Mass., and the other the famous Broadway Tabernacle, in New York City, a church from which he has just recently resigned after a remarkable ministry of more than thirty years.

Dr. Jefferson is always selected when groups of the twenty-five greatest Protestant preachers in the United States are chosen. He is always asked by men who select such volumes as this one to contribute a sermon. He is noted first of all as a great preacher, a man who has specialized in preaching. Second, he is famed as a great executive, who for more than ten years in his first church, and more than thirty years in New York City, has kept the financial and executive affairs of a great city church in fine condition. He is noted, third, as the author of many inspirational books of sermons which may be found in the libraries of young and old preachers all over the United States. He has been a preacher to preachers for years and his books on homiletics and ministerial problems have always been popular with the men of his own profession. If one were to add a fourth characteristic by which Dr. Jefferson is known it would be his passion for Christ. His preaching rings with this great Cathedral-bell note. He is truly a great Evangelist.

The God of the Living

By Charles E. Jefferson, Pastor, Broadway
Tabernacle, New York City

"God is not the God of the dead, but of the living."
—Matt. XXII: 32

THE expansion of the physical universe under the
eye of the modern telescope has weakened in many
thoughtful minds the belief in immortality. In a
universe so vast as ours is now known to be, it seems
absurd to many to assume that a creature so small as
man will live on forever. But this weakening of faith
is of the nature of bewilderment, due to a sudden
access of light, and is not the result of reflection.
Maturer thought will dissipate the fog and restore our
confidence again. The mind has a marvelous capacity
to recover from the shocks which are given it by the
attacks of those who make war on its fundamental beliefs. Through many centuries the doctrine of immortality has been assailed by doubts and misgivings.
Every generation has had its unbelievers who have
formulated arguments against life after death which
have for a season been difficult to answer. But the
eclipse of faith has in every case been transient and
mankind has come back to take up again a belief which

117

it seems incapable of permanently shaking off. One of the most impressive phenomena of history is the fact that the normal human mind is unable to get rid of the belief that when a man dies he lives again.

The universality of this belief is as impressive as its permanence. All races have instinctively believed in a spirit world into which men pass at death. The belief is not confined to one country nor is it peculiar to one race. Primitive man had it and civilized man still retains it as one of his most precious possessions. The animist of Central Africa and the scholar of London or Paris or New York both alike are convinced that death does not end all. If this is a superstition it is one of amazing vitality and grows even stronger in the home of refinement and culture. Many a primitive belief has been sloughed off by the expanding mind, but while "earth outgrows the mythic fancies sung beside her in her youth" this is a fancy which all the races of men refuse to surrender. Any phenomenon which is universal and also persistent earns the right to claim the earnest attention and high respect of all thoughtful men. It is not probable that the human mind is so constructed as perpetually to deceive us. Its constant lurch in the direction of a spirit world in which the soul finds its permanent abode is one of the strongest proofs that such a world is a reality. The chief reason for believing in the reality of the physical universe is the impression which it makes upon our physical senses. This impression is universal and constant. There is another impression made on the mind equally universal and persistent, the conviction that man lives after death, and it is irrational to contend that this conviction is the creation of nothingness, an hallucination or dream which has no vital connection with reality. No one is willing to believe that our eyes and ears and fingers are so made as continuously to deceive us. It is equally difficult to believe that our mind is so made as to lead us perpetually astray in regard to the future which is concealed from us by the tomb.

If man does not live after death then in death he becomes extinct. The idea of extinction sends a chill through the blood. In our weary and discouraged hours we may say we should like to lie down in an eternal sleep, but the mood is an abnormal one and what we say does not report the real conclusion of the mind. When we come to ourself we rejoice in the prospect of going on. It is not what we say when we are sick but what we say when we are well that must be reckoned with in our effort to understand life. As soon as we begin to think and refuse to allow ourself to be swayed by dark feelings, we say with Tennyson:

> Thou wilt not leave us in the dust;
> Thou madest man, he knows not why;
> He thinks he was not made to die;
> And thou hast made him, thou art just.

It is at the grave of a man truly great and good that the heart speaks some of its deepest and most trustworthy words. It is then that the idea of annihilation becomes most abhorrent. At the grave of Jesus, who can believe that death ends all? If death is indeed the end then at the close of a certain day Jesus of Nazareth and Judas Iscariot became equal. Both of them had vanished from the universe in which they had played a brief and ineffectual part. One had been noble and the other had been mean; one had been unselfish and the other had been a traitor, but both received the same reward. There is something in the corpuscles of the blood which revolts against such a suggestion. How did it get there? Who put it there? What does it signify?

If in our darkened hours we hear a voice saying to us, "Believe no more," there is something within us which awakes and "like a man in wrath the heart stands up and answers, 'I have felt.'" There are at least a few men in history whom we will not willingly let die. To us they are alive forevermore. Washington is still living. The supposition that he and Benedict Arnold are nothing today but two hands fulls of dust or that Abraham Lincoln received nothing from God beyond what God granted to Wilkes Booth causes the soul to recoil as from the edge of a sharp knife. There are some things which are unthinkable. In his *Pages from a Journal*, Mr. Hale White relates his experience at the grave of Thomas Carlyle. "Was it possible that such as he could altogether die? Some touch, some turn, I could not tell what or how, seemed all that was necessary to enable me to see and hear him. It was just as if I were perplexed and baffled by a veil which prevented recognition of him, although

I was sure he was behind it." We are so built that we repudiate the doctrine of annihilation.

It is against this impregnable instinct that all the billows of skepticism have beaten in vain. Here is a rock in the structure of man which can never be washed away. All fears of what science may be able to do are groundless. Science knows absolutely nothing concerning what lies beyond death. She has made wonderful progress in many directions within the last fifty years, but she has not progressed a single inch into that strange country from which no traveler returns. When a British scientist of repute says, "At death the spirit of man will be extinguished like a candle flame," he is not talking as a scientist but like an ignorant dogmatist who is asserting as a fact what is nothing but an idle fancy. A scientist, like every other man, has the privilege of conjecturing what takes place at death but no scientist has the right to palm off one of his conjectures as a fact which has been discovered by scientific investigation. There is not a scintilla of evidence brought to light by science to render improbable the survival of the soul. Science has accumulated an enormous mass of interesting and important facts, but not one of them throws light on what happens to the soul when the heart ceases to beat. The scientist possesses no instrument by which he can feel his way out into the darkness of the tomb. There is no microscope by which a scientist can see the soul. There is no telescope by which a scientist can look into heaven. The little telescope used by Galileo told him nothing of the home of the soul, and the new two hundred inch telescope will tell us no more. The anthropologist can tell us nothing, nor can the geologist speak an illuminating word, nor can the physiologist or the chemist or the physicist or the biologist give us authentic information concerning this dim region into which our eyes peer in vain. When a scientist speaks on the subject he must speak as a philosopher and not as a scientist. He has no data which the laboratory has supplied. He possesses no informing facts which his investigations have brought to light. He has nothing but a theory or a speculation, a guess or a wish. For the believer in immortality the latest science has not blocked the way.

The real obstacles to belief in immortality are not those offered by science but are of a different sort. It is difficult for many to believe in the spirit world because they are not able to picture it. Only the picturable to them seems real. The imagination is one of the feeblest of our faculties and when it stands face to face with the world beyond death it is impotent. The mind is abashed and overcome by the multitude of questions it can ask for which there is no answer. Where do our loved ones go at death? Where are they now? What are they doing? Do they know what we are doing? Are they made unhappy by our sorrows? Are they pained by our sins? Are they made glad by our joys? Do they help us in our work? Can we help them by our prayers? With what kind of a body are they clothed? What is the character of their life? These are a few of a thousand questions which surge up in the mind, and alas, no answers are forthcoming. It is because the other world is so silent and so unresponsive to our questions, that many persons are tempted to deny its existence. If it could be described in words they could understand they would believe in it.

But the unpicturableness of the future life is not proof of its non-existence. We are only children and children can always ask more questions than anyone can answer. It does children good to ask questions, and it also does them good to wait for the answer. Sometimes they must wait for years. It will do us no harm to wait until we pass through the gateway of death for answers to these puzzling questions. Paul did not know what kind of a body we are going to have. He called it a spiritual body, a body which would be an adequate instrument for the use of the spirit, but beyond this we know nothing. St. John had keen spiritual vision, but he did not shrink from confessing that it doth not yet appear what we are going to be. All we know is that we are going to approximate the ideal.

It is the foolish efforts of men to picture what cannot be pictured which has put new stumbling blocks in the way of those who want to believe. Pictures of heaven and hell have been great disturbers of the human heart. Descriptions of the home of the blessed have always been tawdry and cheap. In the best heaven ever painted one would not care to stay overnight. Pictures of hell have invariably been grotesque, and most of them disgusting. Men have turned away from them in derision. The incredibility of the pictures has shaken confidence in the spirit world altogether. Virgil and Dante and Milton were great poets but they did not know how to paint a picture of hell. They were dreamers and led men astray by their dreams. The Bible is a sane book. The Old Testament makes no effort to picture either heaven or hell. This helps one to believe that those holy men of old wrote as they were moved by the Holy Spirit. Jesus gave us no pictures of hell or heaven nor did the greatest of his apostles, St. Paul. The imaginative genius who wrote the last book of the New Testament gives us in two or three chapters a fleeting glimpse into the eternal world but his words are all symbols expressing spiritual ideas. When he gives us his picture of the New Jerusalem it is not of a city in the skies but a city on this earth. He does not picture what is going to be on the other side of death. The glorious city is to stand on this side of the grave. The world beyond death is not to be pictured by even the greatest of the saints. Eye cannot see it and ear cannot hear it and heart cannot conceive it. All that we can do is to treasure and enjoy those intimations of it which God gives here and now to those who love him.

In recent years some have been caused to stumble by what certain psychologists have reported. The Witch of Endor has become in certain circles a popular figure and she is able to bring back from the dead not only Samuel but a great host of the departed. What the dead say is so puerile and their chosen methods of communicating their message to their friends in this world are so peculiar that many are led to give up all belief in immortality, convinced it is a doctrine taught by charlatans and believed only by dupes. Up to the present no revelation has come to us from the world of the dead which is of the slightest significance to our generation. Even men who while on earth were preëminent for intellectual power and wisdom, when they attempt to speak to us fall into habits of thought which suggest mental degeneration. If we are to accept as authentic the alleged communications which come from the dead through the most expert of the mediums, it would seem that the dead instead of rising at death to a higher plane of existence have gone down in the scale of being and that the next world is lower than this.

But here again the obstacle is one which the healthy human mind will sweep out of the way. The catastrophe of the World War left a multitude afflicted with shell shock and it is not to be wondered at that the awful grief occasioned by the digging of ten million graves should increase the desire to penetrate the world of the dead to an intensity never before experienced. In times of great mental tension minds often become credulous and beliefs are adopted which later on are cast aside. The fact of immortality cannot be permanently blurred by anything which the Witch of Endor can say or do.

It is because of these obstacles to entire trust in our instincts, that we need the reassuring words of Jesus of Nazareth. In regard to the world beyond death he had no doubts. He was to live after death. He was sure of it. He did not argue it, he knew it. Not only was he to live after death, but his disciples were also to enjoy continued life. He would meet them again. And he did. They were all sure that he did. Because they were sure of this, we have the Christian church. The church is not a theory, it is a fact. It is not a fancy, but an institution. It has been in existence nineteen hundred years. The gates of death have not prevailed against it. It is founded on the resurrection of Jesus. All branches of the church teach the immortality of the soul. They do it because Jesus arose from the dead.

But the church does not build its faith solely on what is written in a book. It builds upon an indestructible instinct. It builds also upon a living experience. The spirit of God bears witness with its spirit that He is not a God of the dead, but of the living. Those who have the spirit of Christ are certain that they shall never die. It is Christ in them which is the hope of glory. The life that is in Christ courses through them. Because he lives they live also.

If the Father of Jesus Christ is indeed the Creator and Ruler of the universe, then extinction becomes unthinkable. If God is our Father He would not deceive us for a few years and then allow us to drop into nothingness. If we are His children and share

His life, we must of course live with Him forever. He is not the God of dead people. He is the God of people who live. If man is annihilated at death then the human race will some day become extinct, and after all the struggle and anguish of human history there will be nothing left but an uninhabited cinder drifting through the deeps of space. God would be a God only of the dead! There would be no hearts to commune with Him, no souls whom He could love. The race for which His only Son died upon the cross would be blown as dust through the cosmic spaces, and God would be alone! It cannot be. Those who say that the soul at death is blown out like a candle are like the ancient Sadducees. They do err not knowing the Scriptures nor the power of God. They do not know the love of God in their own heart. They are not living as Jesus lived and hence cannot understand Jesus' teaching. In our duller hours when the fire of devotion is burning low and our life has taken on a selfish tinge we may play with the ancient question, "If a man die, shall he live again?" and possibly give a negative answer, but when we are walking in the light of the One who is the light of the world all our doubts vanish. When we are in fellowship with Him, we walk in the light and when we are crucified with Him we have no doubt that we shall rise with Him. To be sure of immortality one must live like an immortal.

The Logic of Immortality

BURRIS ATKINS JENKINS,
D.D., Litt.D., LL.D.

Burris Atkins Jenkins was born in
Kansas City, Mo., Oct. 2nd, 1869,
and is still living in that great mid-
western city as a minister in the Linwood Boulevard Christian Church.

One could hardly name the two
men who have had the largest continuous influence in this great mid-
western continent and not name
William Allen White and Dr. Burris Atkins Jenkins, both, in a way
preachers, and both newspaper men.

Burris Atkins Jenkins has distinguished himself in many fields since
he graduated from Bethany College
in 1891 and took an S.T.B. from
Harvard in 1895.

As a War Correspondent during
the World War for *The Kansas City
Star* he wrote some of the most
quoted articles that were published
in America. He has always been
associated with newspapers, having
from 1919 to 1921 been Editor and
publisher of the *Kansas City Journal-
Post*. Even now he is the Editor-
in-Chief and publisher of *The
Christian,* a journal representing the
liberals of the Christian Church. He
is primarily famous, however, as a
great preacher. Since September of

1907 he has preached to capacity audiences in the Christian Church in Kansas City and three times in that period it has been necessary for this organization to build new edifices to handle the crowds.

As a writer Dr. Jenkins has been successful in more than one field. His journalistic bent, already mentioned, led him into the fiction field and he wrote two popular novels "Princess Salome" and "The Bracegirdle." His devotional books and books of sermons are popular with preachers and his column called "The Drift of the Day" which he publishes each week in *The Christian* has recently been put into book form.

The Logic of Immortality

By Burris Atkins Jenkins, Pastor Linwood Christian Church, Kansas City, Mo.

"He is not here, but is risen."
—LUKE XXIV: 6

PEOPLE go to church on Easter who have not gone since the previous one. They decorate homes and sanctuaries with spring flowers, symbols of immortality. They may not know whether they believe in immortality or not; they may even think they do not; and still down deep in their consciousness hold to this larger hope. The Christian world is threaded through, like a tapestry shot with golden thread, with the expectation of immortality and eternal life. I know how many there are who say to themselves—and all of us, no doubt, do at times—"I think a man is a machine, living like the animals, dying like them and returning to the earth and to oblivion when what we call life is done." Nevertheless, underneath these superficial words there lies an inalienable hope which amounts almost to conviction, that if a man die he shall live again and that one day we shall see face to face those whom we have loved long since and lost a while. Most of us do not know how ingrained is our belief in immortality.

Let a time come when death touches those who are most precious to us, wife or child, father or mother, and then that hope comes surging up in us like a powerful rising tide that all our little skepticisms cannot hold back. We do not realize that the idea of man being just a machine is really no different from the belief that he is a living soul; for a machine implies a machinist, and an automaton must have behind it somebody to make it go. It is short-sighted philosophy then to hold a mechanistic conception of the universe, because you have only pushed the creator of it a little further into the background. He is there just the same and has to be. Robert Ingersoll declared himself a skeptic and an agnostic, and no doubt rendered great service by stripping away many an old superstition; but his heart spoke sometimes more clearly than his head, and the most beautiful thing as well as one of the truest that he ever uttered was his little one-minute oration by the side of his brother's dead body in the Capitol at Washington:

"Life is a narrow veil between the cold and barren peaks of two eternities. We strive in vain to look beyond the heights, we cry aloud and the only answer is the echo of our wailing cry. From the voiceless lips of the unreplying dead there comes no word; but in the night of death, hope sees a star and listening love can hear the rustle of a wing."

What I want to do, then, is not to spend time proving or trying to prove immortality. Like God it is too great to be proved, or to require proof. What I do want to do is to assume that deep down in our hearts we all believe in it, with greater or less intensity of faith. We take Jesus at his word when he declared that it *was* so and we believe that somehow, in some form, he arose on that first Easter day and has been almightily alive in the world ever since. What effect does this conviction, conscious or unconscious on our part, have upon our lives? That is what I would like for us to ponder. I maintain that we believe it, whether we believe that we believe it or not. Now then, how does it affect us?

I think it gives us certain qualities, certain virtues. It gives us a certain courage. It enables us to meet the shocks and privations, the strain and the trial, the drama and the tragedy of human life with a degree of bravery, a sort of fortitude. One who is firmly grounded in the hope of an unending life is not so likely to put an end voluntarily to the life that is. It takes a certain courage to snuff out one's life, to be sure, but it takes a far higher courage to stay at his post till the sunset and the dark. Hamlet, in his immortal soliloquy, debates the question as to whether to live or not to live. He cries out:

Who would bear the whips and scorns of time,
The oppressor's wrong, the proud man's contumely,
The pangs of despised love, the law's delay,
The insolence of office, and the spurns
That patient merit of the unworthy takes,
When he himself might his quietus make
With a bare bodkin? Who would fardels bear,

To grunt and sweat under a weary life,
But that the dread of something after death,
The undiscover'd country from whose bourn
No traveller returns, puzzles the will,
And makes us rather bear those ills we have
Than fly to others that we know not of?

Conscience may make cowards; but immortality, brave men. The old religions of fear acted as a deterrent from wrong courses, but the Christian faith in an unending life acts as, an inspiration to do well for right's own sake. And I think all will agree with me that in this so difficult work of living we need courage. Anything that will give us courage, that will make us brave is worth its weight in gold, whether it be a person or an idea. The boys going into battle over on the other side were more afraid of being afraid than of anything else. Most of them, too, summoned to their aid, even though they had little to say about it, the faith of their fathers and the undying hope of immortality. To put it on the lowest ground, then, it pays to believe in a future life. It enables us to walk up to pain, to loss, to old age, to helplessness, to death itself and to say to all of these impostors, "You cannot conquer me; you cannot even get the best of me; your grip upon me is only temporary and passing; for I am immortal."

Again this faith and hope gives us a certain buoyancy, resiliency, a sort of sprightliness and verve, that I really believe characterizes Christian nations. We may be scarcely aware of it, but there is a certain lightness of step and of touch, a certain springiness of nerve and action which, to a degree at least, those who are without our everlasting hope may lack. It is hard to picture this buoyancy and grace; but it was evident among the allied troops in the world war. There were the Roosevelt boys, who as General Harbord tells us, went into Notre Dame Cathedral one day when many people were kneeling there and offering votive candles to different saints. The French churches were much frequented by anxious or hopeless people in war time. These American boys looked on for a while and finally one of them ventured, "Oughtn't we to do something?" They felt an obligation to join in with the French people in their worship and supplications; but they were unacquainted with the saints and scarcely knew where to turn. Finally one of them had a happy thought. Joan of Arc was a saint, she must have a niche or a statue somewhere around here. So they started out to look for it. An old woman volunteered to help and others joined in. They found Joan's niche, they sent for candlesticks and candles; and the populace outside, hearing that there were a couple of American boys doing something in the cathedral, came pouring in to watch, and were delighted beyond measure to see these young chaps lighting candles before St. Joan, who had not been recognized by anybody else.

Again, there was General Pershing who gave frequent illustrations of what I mean by buoyancy and spirited bearing. Whether that phrase, "Lafayette, we are here," is authentic or not, it certainly is true that when our General first visited the tomb of Napoleon at the Hôtel des Invalides, as he stood uncovered in that solemn resting place of the greatest soldier in the world, an old crippled veteran of 1870, keeper of the tomb, came bringing Napoleon's sword, borne tenderly upon his two hands, and extended it for General Pershing to take and handle. Ninety-nine military men out of a hundred would have taken it by the hilt and tried it in the hand. Not so this one hundredth man. Drawing himself up rigidly, his hands at his sides, he bent forward from the hips and reverently kissed the handle of the sword. The French people loved him for that. It was grace, buoyancy, resiliency.

Some say we are a sad people. If so we hide it well, under an exterior of mirth and joyousness. We give the impression to older nations of a vast supply of springiness and verve. According to Mr. Kipling, this American spirit says of the American citizen, "Mine ancient humour saves him whole."

Then this hope of immortality gives us an all-round faith in ourselves, in life, in the world in which we live. One cannot belittle himself when conscious that he is immortal. One cannot sincerely call himself a poor worm of the dust. On the contrary he knows that he is infinitely valuable to Him who made him. Jesus impressed that on us. Whatever else we can say about man, we know that he is the highest artistry of God, the most complicated and beautiful of all the machines that the great Machinist has made.

And we have a profounder faith in life, mixed up as it is, and all at sixes and sevens. We know that justice does not reign in the imperfect circle of our years. We suffer as much for what we have not done as through any fault of our own. Few men get their just desserts in this world either for good or ill. Consciously or unconsciously, however, we cherish the belief that some day all sixes and sevens will be straightened out, and that justice shall reign, that right shall be all in all, and that perfect peace and perfect happiness we shall surely attain. We cannot conceive of an endless life that is imperfect, open to injustice, filled with evil.

> We can but trust that good will fall
> At last far off at last to all
> And every winter turn to spring.

This hope, too, gives us faith in the world. It has a purpose; there is a plan back of it and a planner. I have already hinted how hard it is to believe that there is no such personality back of all—much harder than to believe that there is. Is there evil in the city and the Lord hath not done it? This philosophizing of the old Hebrew saint and sage is good straight thinking. We know there is evil in the world and we don't know why. We shall never know why until some day we see face to face and eye to eye and understand. We shall never solve the problem of this evil, but assuming that we are immortal and shall live eternally at home with the Father, the Creator, the Force, the

Personality back of it all, we are willing to wait for the solution and able to wait.

Greater faith in one another too, follows hard upon the endless hope. As we are immortal, dignified, valuable, so we know that our fellow human beings are the same, precious in the sight of their God. We cannot, therefore, hold lightly or cheaply the personality of an eternal life, that walks by our side. Humanity may seem to us at times never so unlovely, so stupid, so perverse. We may cry out with Puck, "What fools these mortals be!" None the less, with all their foolishness they are immortal lives, undying souls. They seem to us stupid, foolish or vicious, just because we do not know what goes on within their breasts. "To know all is to forgive all," says an old French proverb. It is fair and full of wisdom. Every individual human being wants to do right, wants nothing else quite so much, wants to develop to the highest perfection of which he is capable, wants to live out a worthy destiny. He thinks he is taking the right means to this self-expression and self-development. He may be taking just the wrong one, but that is the fault of his judgment and not his will to do right. We cannot, therefore, hold a low estimate of our fellowman and at the same time hold the belief, no matter how dim and uncertain, in the immortal destiny of that fellowman.

Then it gives, too, a faith in God. People are uncertain, very uncertain, about God and their ideas of Him, their view, their thought of Him. This is certain, that if we hold hard to the faith in immortality, indulge ourselves in this so strengthening and inspiring bright hope, we shall enable ourselves the better to understand our Heavenly Father and to trust Him and to surrender to Him. As a little child believes implicitly in his mother and his father even though he cannot understand them, what they say, what they do, what they are driving at, so does a child of the Eternal believe that He does all things well, that He has a definite purpose, and that purpose a good and beneficent one. "Thy will be done" becomes the prayer of surrender and unfaltering trust which is linked up with the faith in an endless life.

I have already anticipated the next result of a belief in immortality, and that is the increased valuation placed on human life by those who indulge in this hope. The one who sees no future beyond the grave, to whom death ends all, will logically end in holding human life cheap and all but valueless. He will not hesitate to override another and to grind him down, to make cannon fodder of him or factory fodder. He will work little children at the spindles of great cotton mills and let them grow old before their time and die in herds before middle life to forward his own selfish purposes. He may even think that he believes in the eternal destiny of each one of these little children. He may say the creed in his church service Sunday after Sunday, but his faith is very shallow and his hope is very dim. An abiding conviction in the immortality of every child, no matter how humble and obscure, results inevitably in a high valuation of that little life. Nations which throw men's lives away by the millions to gain empire and dominance and trade have simply allowed their hope of endless life to grow dim. The higher that hope burns, the farther its light will be shed into the homes and the hearts of the humblest citizens for they are children of the Most High and destined to everlasting life.

A final effect of our belief in immortality is the kindling of aspiration in the hearts of men and women. The more we believe that life begins here and goes on and on and has no end, the more we shall desire to live the finest and the best life of which we are capable here and now looking forward to a growth and an expansion throughout the endless reaches of eternity. A hopeless man just naturally can't be an aspiring man. The less hope he has the more will he sink down into a slough either of contentment or of despond.

And aspiration it is after all that saves us men and women. It is not so much what we are as what we want to be that counts. As a matter of fact, just as a father takes the will for the deed with his child, so does our Heavenly Father take our aspiration for achievement. This is only putting into more modern language St. Paul's old doctrine of justification by faith. He tells us that God takes the faith of Abraham and counts it to him for righteousness, and that so He takes the faith of each one of us, and reckons it to us as performance. By which I think he means, of course, that God counts our will for the deed, that He accepts our aspiration as if it were success; for as some modern poet has said, "What we honestly and sincerely aspire to be, that in some sense we are." The more we look upon life as an immortal endowment, the more we shall seek to improve the time that we have here to fit ourselves to the best advantage for a good start in what we call that other life. Ambition, aspiration mark the devout believer in the Lord Christ and in his doctrine of immortality.

It is for us, then, to cherish that hope, to fan the flame of it, to build it up with all possible fuel until it shall rise higher and higher, clear and plain and strong. As we do we shall grow in courage, in buoyancy, in faith in ourselves, in life, in one another, in the world and in God. We shall value human life for what it is, the highest and finest work of God; and we shall aspire to make that life as far as in us lies a thing of beauty and of joy. He who was raised on Easter day has given us this firm hope. He and no other has taught us without the shadow of doubt that we shall meet again after separation and shall enter into endless peace. Thank God for this bright message, this happy truth.

If I Had One Sermon to Preach on Immortality

HARRY LEVI

Harry Levi is one of the most famous of Jewish preachers in the United States. He was born in Cincinnati, Ohio, August 7th, 1875, graduating from the Hebrew Union College, Cincinnati, Ohio, in 1897, the same year he was ordained to the ministry. He was a Rabbi in Wheeling, West Virginia, from 1897 to 1911 and since then has been the pastor of Temple Israel, Boston, Mass.

He is a Mason and a member of B'nai B'rith, belongs to the Boston City Club, and is the author of *Jewish Characters in Fiction.*

Harry Levi is, in addition to being a most distinguished clergyman in his own church, popular as a lecturer in college circles, Lyceum and Chautauqua. He is one of the best known clergymen in the city of Boston, where his great church is crowded with people Sunday after Sunday, winter and summer.

He is frequently quoted in the newspapers of his city and in the publications of his own denominations. He lives in Brookline, Mass.

If I Had One Sermon to Preach on Immortality

By HARRY LEVI, TEMPLE ISRAEL, BOSTON, MASS.

"Though he slay me, yet will I trust in him."
—JOB XIII: 15

No one has ever returned from beyond the grave. All through the ages men have tried to pierce the veil of the further world, but unsuccessfully. A whole host of writers has described in detail the conditions supposed to obtain in heaven. All this has been imagination run riot. Spiritualistic mediums have asserted that they could communicate with the dead. But most of them have been and are frauds. As for the rest, belief has outstripped evidence. When a Sir Oliver Lodge and a Conan Doyle tell us of their experiences, we must perforce listen reverently. Who dare say they are deluded or that their conclusions are impossible and incredible? When that which is ridiculed one day becomes the reality of the next, when we think of the manner in which so many fanciful dreams have been realized, and so many prophecies fulfilled, which long seemed the expressions of disordered minds, when we think of steamships and submarines and aeroplanes and wireless and radios, who dare say anything is impossible?

IF I HAD ONLY ONE SERMON TO PREACH

There are more things in heaven and earth,
Than are dreamt of in your philosophy . . .

So long as faith was mere credulity, a capacity to believe anything, not only that which is unproven but which cannot be proven, that which contradicts reason and violates the canons of intelligence, anyone could accept the belief in immortality. Nowadays however, men are not content to accept dogmas just because their parents stood loyally by them, nor because their particular church preaches them. They demand proof. But what proof have we for immortality? And how explain the fact that in the face of this meager proof we still believe in immortality? Is it merely a matter of the wish being father to the thought? We want to live on. We love life. We dread the feeling that death ends all. Do our yearnings compel us to a hope which at best remains only a hope? Have we no ground for our faith, nothing to offer which will lift our desire to the realm of reality? Why do I believe in everlasting life?

First because the belief is so old. Of course age is no proof of truth. There are lies which are hoary with years. Sometimes knowledge grows from more to more slowly. There are still those who hold and teach beliefs that are wholly contrary to fact. It is difficult if not impossible to read books like Dorsey's *Why We Behave Like Human Beings*, or Robinson's *The Mind in the Making* or Seabrook's *Magic Island* without realizing how many superstitions which can

146

have no basis in fact, people still entertain. But if there is anything to the doctrine of the survival of the fittest, then while some lies and mistakes may linger long before they go, it would be inconceivable that such a belief as that in everlasting life should have persisted through the ages without warrant. Grant that as the ages have come and gone we have learned much which the people of long ago did not know, that in some respects our children are better informed than were our ancestors. Yet these people of all the bygone ages were not illiterates, ignorant men and women, easily deceived. Nor were they all uneducated. There were wise men among them, and thinkers and philosophers. And they too believed in immortality. An old teacher of mine once remarked that "what the world in general believes to be true is apt to be true" and that is so.

Nor is this attitude merely a matter of yesterday. Do we live in an intelligent, educated day? Are we less easily deceived or persuaded than were our progenitors? Do we decline to believe unless we have proof, some evidence that satisfies not simply our emotional but our intellectual needs? Yet most people even of today believe in immortality. And once again, not merely the unlettered, nor yet pious, trusting, unquestioning church-goers, but the thinkers of our day. Here is a recent volume, *We Believe in Immortality*, edited by Sydney Strong, and published by Coward-McCann Inc. The volume contains the statements of some one hundred men and women defining their attitude toward the question of immortality. All prominent men and women, conspicuous men and women, men and women known for their independent thinking, for the intellectual positions they occupy, business men, philosophers, poets, educators, writers. Here are the confessions of intellectuals like Roger Babson, Alice Stone Blackwell, Henry Churchill King of Oberlin, Charles Thwing of Western Reserve University, David Starr Jordan of Leland Stanford, Charles Little, until recently of Michigan University, John Hibben of Princeton, Mary E. Woolley of Mt. Holyoke, Elbert Russel of Duke, Daniel Marsh of Boston University, Elmer Brown of New York University, W. H. P. Fawce of Brown, Margaret Deland, Dr. Cadman, John J. Tigert, Commissioner of Education, Edward A. Filene, S. O. Levinson of Chicago, the great authority on international peace, Robert Milliken, Vida Scudder. No mean or inconspicuous names these. Yet with hardly an exception, the whole list admits its beliefs in immortality. They differ in details of course. Nor do they agree in the reasons for their belief. But the point is they agree in holding the belief. If such distinguished men and women are persuaded of the reality of immortality, must there not be something to the belief, something to warrant our own interest and acceptance?

Most of us believe in God. But if God is, then He must be just. And if God be just, I cannot conceive that He would permit men and women, of every generation and age, from the most primitive times to our own day, to share a belief of this character, to retain a passionate loyalty to it, unless somehow it bespeaks objective reality. We may "fool some of the people all the time and all the people some of the time, but never all the people all the time." And "God is not a man that He should lie." "On the earth the broken arcs; in the heaven a perfect round." Wherefore Arthur Smith could properly ask "can it be fancied that deity ever vindictively made in His image a mannikin merely to madden it?" Can our belief in everlasting life be only self-deceit? If so, where is God?

"To pitch this life high," said Samuel Crothers, "does it not mean to develop all the nobler powers and trust them to the uttermost? Thus the man has lived. At last the moment comes when life strikes hard on death. For that moment, too, comes the word, 'pitch this one high.' That means that he is to summon his best, that he is to keep on as aforetime with his face toward the light—he is to keep on—hoping, loving, daring, aspiring. And then comes the sudden silence, and to us who watch the brave ongoing all things seem possible. All things seem possible save that there should be no path for these patient feet."

If God be just, it is incredible that here on earth we should know so much of spiritual life, so much of aspiration and idealism, so much of love, the desire to serve, the capacity for self-sacrifice, so much of courage and heroism, expressions which grow in in-

tensity and adequacy as the years advance, it is incredible that all this should find such development
while we are here, to issue suddenly in nothingness,
in futility, just because our bodies go into the grave.
It may be difficult to believe in immortality. But
how much more difficult to believe in complete, human, spiritual, annihilation?

We believe in evolution. We accept as a working
hypothesis the theory that all life has gradually, definitely, inevitably evolved from the simplest and
humblest beginnings. Certain details may still be
lacking. Complete proof may not be at hand. But
practically all thinkers agree that evolution represents
a fact. We feel assured of physical evolution, and of
mental evolution. We have before our eyes proof of
moral evolution. Why not spiritual evolution? If
the soul has evolved through the ages, why should this
evolution suddenly come to an end? Why should it
not go on even beyond the grave? Drummond writes
of *Natural Law in the Spiritual World*. Why not?
Why doubt that there is a spiritual world? And how
can spiritual life come to an end?

Science assures us that nothing ever can really disappear. It may pass beyond our physical vision. But
it can never cease to be. Water may evaporate. Coal
may be dissolved into its constituent elements and become invisible. It simply changes its form. That is
true of everything in the universe. Why should it be,
how can it be true of everything in the universe save
that which represents the highest expression of uni-

versal life, the soul of man? If the whole of life is merely a series of transformations, why is not, why must not what we call death, be but a part of the series?

The changes of nature which thrust themselves upon us wherever we turn compel us to this conclusion. Winter is always followed by spring. Death which hovers over all of outdoor life during the wintry months becomes new life as the cold season goes. Night always gives way to dawn. Here is no end, only change. God is true to physical nature. Shall He be less true to man, as yet the highest expression of His creative power and will and wisdom? "There is no death, what seems so is transition."

Once again, if God be just, immortality must be reality. While we live we encounter so many instances of apparent injustice. Good men die young. Vile men live to a ripe old age. Little children are carried away before they have had a chance to achieve, before they have known youth, before they have really lived. Men of ability go long ere they have been able to exhaust their talent, often indeed on the verge of doing greater things than they have ever known. Virtue here often finds only poverty and vice wealth. Courage is often rewarded with misunderstanding and hatred and abuse. If there is a God, and God is just, as we all believe, then the life we know here cannot be all. Somewhere, beyond the grave, must be opportunity for the fulfillment we could not find here. Somewhere children and men must have the chance to complete that which here they left incomplete. Somewhere beyond the grave we shall all find that which we are denied here. Wisely John Fisk once remarked "I believe in the immortality of the soul as the supreme act of faith in the reasonableness of God's work."

All of which of course is mere inference. We cannot prove immortality as one proves a mathematical proposition. But then how little proof we have for any belief. We live in every direction by faith, that faith which I like to feel is not credulity, but inference based on experience, our experience or that of the race. We actually know so little, yet we venture so daringly, building our towering structures on a faith we trust will not disappoint us. Who can prove the stability of the earth? Yet contractors and architects are not deterred from rearing their sky-scrapers by the meagerness of their data. Who can prove the inevitability of the laws of nature? We have seen nature express itself in certain ways, we have generalized from this evidence and for the rest have hoped that our conclusions were correct and that nature would not fail us. And thus far it has not failed us. We believe in God, but no one has seen God "face to face." We believe in Him because of the work He has done, because of all He has left behind Him. We cannot otherwise interpret the universe. All that we see about us, all that we experience, compels us to the belief in God.

And so we believe in immortality. No one has ever returned from the grave. But wherever we turn we

come upon scenes and situations, we come upon experiences, we come upon evidences that have no meaning save as we believe in immortality. Life is chaotic,
unreasonable, unintelligent, without rhyme or reason,
unless we live forever.

But while hearsay may make for belief, it is personal
experience that determines conviction. I have been a
minister thirty-two years. Over and over again I have
been called to the bedside of those passing away. I
have never seen a dying person afraid. When the
World War was on, Temple Israel sent one hundred
three young men to the front. While they were away
I corresponded with them regularly. How danger
wrought changes in these young men! How it altered
and matured their beliefs and convictions, their vision!
I am persuaded that when we come into the presence
of death we develop a sixth sense that helps us see
far across the great divide, that gives us a vision we
never know under normal circumstances. The nearer
we come to death, the more we find of eternal life, and
the more certain we may be of its reality.

So nothing that I have ever read or been told, nothing that I ever thought, gave me such assurance of
the certainty of everlasting life, as this close, intimate
touch with men and women who stood on the verge
of the great beyond. Washington Gladden once urged
that the best way to prove the truth of immortality is
to live as though it were a fact and everything we
do will demonstrate the validity of the belief. So life
may justify our hope. But the hour when life ends

justifies it even more. How often men are at their best when their days on earth are numbered! The body is almost ready for the grave when the soul knows its furthest reach and its finest vision. At best the body keeps poor pace with the soul. Grant its marvelous capacities, how inadequate it is as an instrument for the expression of all that the soul plans to do and aspires to be. How our ideals outstrip our capacity to realize them. And then there comes the time, when we are relieved of the hampering means through which, while we live here, we have to make known our desires. Stripped then of all that checked and inhibited it, the soul, freed for finer and larger work, gives itself more efficiently than ever to its divine tasks. That is what we call death. We should call it life. For it is the beginning of the larger life.

Why should death be the end? We may destroy a magnificent canvas upon which a great artist impressed his soul, but we do not disturb the artist. We may even give his brushes and colors to the flames without affecting him. We may burn the manuscripts of a great composer, and the composer may never know it. We may reduce to splinters the instrument of a great virtuoso, without in the least touching his genius. We may batter into bits a wireless outfit, a telephone, a radio, and leave those who use them, those who own them, the inventors who conceived them, the men who made them, wholly unharmed. The body may return to the dust whence it came, and the soul

be none the worse, nay even the better for the separation.

I believe in personal immortality and therefore in
personal identity beyond the grave. What gives us
our identity here on earth? Our bodies? Not at all.
What distinguishes each and every one of us is our
personality, that spiritual entity that makes us what
we are, stamps us, marks us as individuals. If this
invisible, spiritual something, which for want of a
better term we call individuality, personality, soul, if
this being can make for identity here, can indeed know
identity here, why should it be otherwise beyond the
grave? Why must spirit lose its individuality simply
because many of us find it difficult to visualize it in
disembodied form? And if the soul retains its identity, why may we not entertain the comforting hope
that one day we shall again see and know the com-
panionship of those we have loved and lost?

What becomes of the soul after death, of course
no one can say. For all we know, the souls of all
who have gone, are hovering about us, trying vainly
to communicate with us by way of a spirit language
we have not as yet mastered. Strange? Why? Mu-
sicians, philosophers, poets often speak a language unintelligible to most of us. God speaks always and
yet few of us hear and understand. Why should we
not some day learn to converse with our dead?

We know nothing of heaven. But wherever it may
be, and whatever, surely heaven must mean an opportunity not only for larger and better work and larger

and happier life, but for a continuance on a higher level of the better interests we know here. Mary Austin never doubts the certainty of a future life, yet sometimes she does fear that in the hereafter she may not know the green fields, the dear old house and the old friends she loves so well. What were heaven without the love, the loved things and the loved men and women who make life even here, so sweet and satisfying?

But if everlasting life means beyond the grave a continuance of the life we know here, then it were well that while we are here we should prepare as well as we can for what is to come afterwards. "The commandments of God were given us to live by and not to die by," said a wise sage of the long ago. Let us live well by them, that the hour of death may find us ready.

It is well that now and then we give this whole matter our earnest consideration. The thought of death may help us pray "Teach us so to number our days that we may get us a heart of wisdom." And it is well that we strive to develop some definite attitude toward the whole question, attain to some settled conviction on the subject. At any rate, even though we come upon no assured opinions, the subject is too important for us to refuse to concern ourselves with it. Only we must not become dogmatic. The wisest of us knows so little. And we who feel we know so much, may be altogether in the wrong. Under no circumstance, if we can help it, should we worry or fear.

IF I HAD ONE SERMON TO PREACH

E. S. Kiser, the poet, gives us wise counsel when he says:

> Why should I sit in doubt or fear? If I
> Awake some morning from that dreaded sleep
> To find myself new-born and lifted high
> Then I will turn, and, looking o'er the deep
> That lies beneath me, shout for joy and throw
> A last good-by at Pain and Fear, below.
> But what if, at the last, no light shall break—
> If this is all—if when I fall asleep
> No angel's voice shall sweetly cry, "Awake,"
> And there shall be but Nothing, dark and deep—
> Oh, well, I shall not care if it be so,
> I'll triumph still, for I shall never know.[1]

But whether we know or not, whether when we go we find light or darkness, while we live, let us so live, that when the hour comes, we shall go unafraid, unashamed, comforted by the consciousness that we deserve well whatever we receive, that we have lived to the best of our ability, that we leave all who belong to us here a heritage that will give them pride and not disappointment, and that all who know us and have been served by us, will have reason to rise and call us blessed.

[1] Used by permission.

Intelligible Immortality

FRANCIS J. McCONNELL, D.D., Litt.D., LL.D.

Francis J. McConnell, now President of the Federal Council of Churches of Christ in America, was born in Trinway, Ohio, August 18th, 1871, graduated at Ohio Wesleyan University in 1894 and at Boston University School of Theology in 1897, taking his Ph.D. from the same University in 1899 under the famous Philosopher, Dr. Borden Parker Bowne, a biography of whom he has just published during the past year.

He entered the Methodist ministry in 1894 and served several small churches, being elected President of DePauw University, a small mid-Western college in 1909. He served here until 1912 when the Methodist General Conference at Baltimore in 1912 elected him a Bishop of the Methodist Episcopal Church.

He has become famous as the editor of the United States Steel Strike Report which brought about the eight hour a day wage scale, as a battler for social and industrial justice, as one of the keenest minds in the church world, as a great college executive, a strong Bishop, a prolific writer of books, a lecturer of repute, deeply emotional in his public utterances, one time Bishop of the Denver Area, then of the Pittsburgh Area, and now of the New York Area.

He has represented his church in Porto Rico, Mexico, and France. During the World War Bishop McConnell served as a Y. M. C. A. speaker along the English, French and American lines. He spoke in the American Church in Paris the first Sunday the "Big Bertha" began to fire on Paris.

He is the author of *Public Opinion and Theology, The Preacher and the People, Is God Limited?* and other popular books. His present address is 150 Fifth Avenue, New York City.

Intelligible Immortality

By FRANCIS J. MCCONNELL, NEW YORK CITY

IF I had only one sermon to preach on immortality, I do not think I would trouble myself much with the formal scientific or logical considerations for or against the belief. Members of various psychical research societies have now and again told us of scientifically verifiable testimony as to the persistence of life after death, but the evidence is scanty at best,—and even if it could be accepted at face value, would often leave us with the question as to whether such continued existence would be desirable. Some twenty-five years ago, when spiritualistic phenomena were attracting large attention in Boston, a medium declared that he was materializing Phillips Brooks. The great preacher's salutation to the audience was: "How are you fellows out there?" which would seem to indicate that the transformation in the Brooks style of speech had been quite complete. Most of the more credible and worthy evidence of survival advanced by the psychic research societies is of such a nature as to be explicable on other suppositions than that of the survival of the persons who have passed from us. I do not by this intend to disparage scientific research through intelligent and responsible channels. All that

I am saying is that if I were to preach on immortality, I should not think it worth while to spend much time on scientific proofs.

And I certainly would not give much time to scientific disproofs—for the simple reason that there are not any such disproofs worth the paper on which they are written. The most that can be said is that the mental activities are dependent on bodily activities, for it cannot be said that there is any way of explaining a thought-process in terms of body process. Everything material moves, or is, in space. A thought may not be possible till a particle of brain-tissue moves up or down, to the right or left, or forward or back, but thoughts themselves are not up or down, to the right or left, or forward or back. A thought has the power to hold things together in a logical fashion which has nothing to do with space terms. We say of one man's argument that it is more forceful than another, but the force we are thinking of is not to be measured in foot-pounds. We are thinking of another order of energy—that of ideas. No rearrangement of brain particles could ever necessarily give us thought. The arrangement might be the condition on which thought took place, but the arrangement moves according to its own laws and thought according to its laws. Suppose messages from the material world outside of our bodies could be actually printed on our brain substance. That would be just the beginning and not the end. Progress toward the end desired—the understanding of the message—could only arise as some agent began to read the message. The outside world does not print itself directly on our brains, and if it did there would have to be some set of measures used for true estimate. To use the old saying, "the thought of a mile is never a mile long." The outside world could only print itself on our brains in miniature, and then would have to give us a key by which to interpret the outside distances aright. All I mean to say is that the connection between body and mind is not such as to make us believe that mind could not conceivably go on without bodies as we see them in this earthly existence. Science cannot prove that thought is necessarily caused by body. The door is open for us to believe in another life so far as anything science can say,—not a wide door, but wide enough,—and open.

The formal logician comes and tells us that the great argument for immortality is that souls are simple substances and therefore indestructible. All the materials that we see around us are combinations. Their destruction means pulling them to pieces. The child gets hold of the father's watch and destroys it by taking it apart. Even after we reach the chemical elements like gold we have not reached final simplicity, for an atom of gold is a little solar system, so to speak, with negatively charged electrons flying around a positively charged proton. If we could knock one of those negatively charged electrons out of the little solar system which we call an atom of gold, we could destroy that particle as gold,—conceivably making it into something else. Now the soul, the logician tells us, is no such complexity. It shows itself in many ways, but it cannot be taken apart. It is indestructible.

But even though it is simple why might not its powers die down? Simple though it is, why might it not get tired and quit? If it had a beginning, it may conceivably have an ending. "Ah," says the apostle of logical exactness, "there's the rub! Or there isn't the rub,—whichever you like. The soul will have no ending because it never had a beginning. It is simple, indestructible, eternal." Well! Well! Then what was I, a little over a half-century ago before I turned up on this bank and shoal of time? Our logical reasoner answers, legitimately enough, that such a question is none of his business. I fear that it is none of mine either, for if I have been existing from all eternity without being aware of the fact what is the difference between such existence and none at all? Self-consciousness and memory are the heart of existence for me, and without those I don't see what advantage there is in my having a core of metaphysical indestructibility. It will be remembered that some years ago Dr. McTaggart, an able philosopher, argued for immortality of just this barren sort. The soul in any stage of existence lives according to the laws of that stage, without ever becoming conscious, except through logical reasoning, that it has ever lived through any succession of stages. Which is about what the ordinary man would mean by personal annihilation at the close of a particular stage. Still, I am not railing against the McTaggarts. I am merely saying that I don't think they would help much in my single sermon on immortality.

We may get an angle of approach to the sermon by asking what conditions would make immortality desirable. I heard a reputable thinker say recently that it is not necessary to believe in God in order to believe in immortality. I doubt if immortality apart from God would be attractive to many of us. Of course, if by some inescapable law of its own nature the universe is just moving on-and-up in an increasingly glorious evolution without the help of a God, and without the need of one, immortality might be worth while, but what reason have we to believe that such an impersonal evolution would be on-and-up? On-and-up is all right, but what about around-and-around? From what we see of the forces of the world which seem most to suggest the impersonal, they are more prone to go around-and-around. Now going around-and-around, even if it is free from positively disagreeable features such as pain of body or spirit, becomes an unspeakable bore. Who craves for an eternity of boredom?

Coming to close quarters with the problem, the only basis for belief in an immortality worth while is belief in a moral God,—the God revealed in Christ. It is the glory of the Old Testament that the writers no sooner got hold of a new moral insight binding for man than they held to that insight as binding for God also,—and thus they set forth through the centuries an increasingly moral conception of God,—a conception in which prophets, lawmakers, poets, seers, and the corporate life of devoted groups, each played their part. On all this as a foundation was revealed the final glory in Jesus Christ.

Before we come to the climax in Jesus, however, suppose we look at some of the more elementary features of the moral in God's character wrought out in the Old Testament. We would not for an instant set moral qualities over against one another, or arrange them higher or lower in a scale. Nevertheless, the Scriptures make it plain that the love revealed in Christ, which God gives to men and seeks from men, is based upon moral fairness and justice. The pivotal question in the Old Testament is that of Abraham: "Shall not the Judge of all the earth do right?" The spirit of a ruler can never be proved in any formal sense. It has to be taken on trust. If the trusting mind finds that the total experience following such trust leads to fuller life,—to mental peace and increased power of will,—the trust will continue. Now the primary consideration in thinking of a moral God is justice. On that basis where does a denial of immortality for men leave God? Taking the race as a whole, throughout its entire history, the majority of men who have lived on earth have never had a human chance. Probably the most of them have never known for any considerable periods the satisfaction of enough to eat. Now one type of mind will say in the presence of this race-old tragedy that the facts which I admit are the most cogent possible proof that there is no God, but another type is not thinking in terms of proof, and holds on in trust awaiting more light. There is nothing especially scientific or reasonable or sensible in passing sentence against God, or against belief in Him, till we have heard all He has to say.

It may be alleged that I am chiefly concerned here with the character of God. I am. I freely admit that there are many persons who say that they are not interested in the question of eternal existence. They say that they have had enough of life at its best. "The fire sinks low and we are ready to depart." Judging by their own experience they avow that they cannot find any race-wide demand of humanity for immortality. Even the longing for loved ones, acute at the moment of separation, softens at last to a hallowed memory which the resumption of actual living contacts might disturb. Let us do the best we can, call it a day, and go to sleep.

The avowal of such an easy-going attitude, however, does not release the Almighty from the obligations of creatorship. An old-time Methodist theologian, who was preaching divine mercy, was once reproached with the remark that if he did not cease talking so much about the divine mercy, he would make hell tolerable; whereupon he replied that he was not especially concerned about making hell tolerable but that he was mightily concerned about making the idea of God tolerable. I assume that these sermons are being written for readers who believe in God. If

that assumption is correct, it becomes of vast importance to them as to what kind of God they believe in.
Christianity believes in a moral God. That belief is
the distinctive mark of Christianity. Morality, in
Christian terms, demands that power be used under a
sense of responsibility. Now if God brought men
into this world without their consent,—and obviously
they could not be consulted beforehand,—He is under
obligation to give them every chance at the fullest and
best life possible. That earthly conditions fall far
short of giving such chance is apparent at a glance.
If this earth is all God can do for me, then the question—not at all irreverent—becomes pertinent—why
do anything at all? If God has the power which He
is conceived of as having in Christian thinking, He
can give men fuller and better life than this. If He
does not have the power, He has to meet the Christian
question as to how He could send the race forth into
a gale like this earthly existence without enough power
to carry men through to something better.

I know there is a type of believer to whom all this
will seem very offensive. To such believers faith
comes easily and naturally. Any questions of this
order seem irreverent and even blasphemous. We are
under obligations, however, if we are taking the idea
of God seriously, to draw out the moral implications
of the idea,—and that is all I am trying to do. Let
us not forget that the challenge of God by moral
standards has been one of the most powerful agents
for Christian progress. Such challenge meant the

death-knell of the old Calvinism,—as it means, on the other hand, the death-knell of all those amiable, easy-going conceptions of God which represent Him as smilingly indulgent toward all the stupidities and monstrosities of our present so-called self-expression. I am not saying that any human being has a right to declare just what in detail a chance at the fullest and best human life involves. All I do say is, that taking the history of the race up to date, it calls for more than any large number of men—large, I mean, as compared with the total of the earth's population— have ever had on earth. I insist that I am keeping close to the Christian idea of God. I am not writing for atheists, or for those who believe in a finite God of such a type that He himself has not yet got himself pulled far enough loose from limitations to be of much service to anyone else.

Enough of the Christian obligations of justice as binding as the Christian God. Suppose we think now of the Christian scheme of values as holding good for God. What are the values which we on earth hold supreme? I suppose I shall not go far astray in listing them as goodness, truth and beauty. Probably few avowed atheists would today deny that these are the chief values, though they would insist on defining them concretely in their own terms. For the Christian the values are these virtues as made actual in the lives of men according to the life in Christ. The glory of men, according to the Christ-ideal, is that they are capable of being endlessly improved. It would seem to be a strange universe, to say nothing of a strange God, that would make it impossible for them to fulfill their possibilities of development.

It is a commonplace in Christianity that men are the ends-in-themselves, so far as earthly creatures are concerned. We have heard time and again that we can think meanly of man as science describes him, or as history records his deeds, but we can never think meanly of man as Christ looks at him. As a matter of fact a considerable volume of the thinking of the past hundred years or so concedes the value of man as an end-in-himself. Going back no further than the eighteenth century we find Kant teaching in imperishable utterance that a man cannot be looked upon as an instrument or tool,—that he has final value on his own account. The French Revolution, irreligious as it was, stood for the same ideal,—though using the more abstract term "humanity." Even materialistically inclined movements like Marxian socialism have practically made men ends-in-themselves. Today laborers are willing to strike not merely for higher wages, but for a more human relationship in shops and factories which will treat them as men rather than as "hands." The current humanistic movement likewise makes men the supreme values,—even though by curious and freakish logic it seeks to make man mean the most for this life by denying the possibility of another life,—and to make him supreme by ruling out God.

Present-day tendencies apart, however, Christianity unmistakably puts man at the center of all earthly values. This does not mean that the physical universe was made solely for man but it does mean that man is of more value than anything physical. Those humble souls, who, following the lead of Herbert Spencer half a century ago, tell us how superior the speed of light is to any human activity, seem to forget that the light apart from a human activity is a mere physical vibration "in the dark,"—that what gives light its glory is the mind of man,—and that the mind of man is the only earthly creature that has the power to measure the speed of light. Man is of more value than many sparrows,—and than many light rays.

On the assumption that the earthly life ends all, what becomes of these human values? One man tells us that they have value to themselves,—that life is supremely sweet. Which raises the question as to why it should stop just about the time when we have begun to appreciate its sweetness. Another man might say that the values are for others as well as for the living men themselves,—but those others also pass away. It is true that the record of the achievements of successive generations becomes more impressive as we go along, but each generation has only time for a glimpse at these glories and then it too must fail. The last generation, before the curtain finally falls, will presumably get a chance to see the whole picture, but who knows but by the time that generation arrives earthly conditions may have become so severe as to leave no time for looking at pictures? If the human values are all treasured up in the vision of God and endure there as memories,—well, all we can say is that such a God is not the Father of our Lord Jesus Christ. If men are the fairest fruit earth can produce, we can hardly think of the God of Christianity as allowing that fruit to fall to the ground and rot. This would argue an obliviousness to values which we cannot reconcile with the character of the God of Christ.

There is space for just a word more, but that word is the most important. I am convinced of the validity of what I have thus far said, but what I have said has not reached the highest Christian plane. We reach that plane when we think of Jesus' thought of God as father. Who of us that is a father would, if he had the power to keep his children living, allow them to sink into nothingness? The question answers itself. If this life is all, we may as well say that we cannot use the word "father" as applied to God in any intelligible sense. Of course, there are devout souls who avow that they are so consecrated to the will of God that if that will calls for the loss of their personal identity they are content. An old teacher of mine,—a high authority in his line,—used always to be saying that with moving unction. It is only fair to comment that his line was not one which called for close reasoning about moral principles and their implications. Such a remark may indicate a degree of grace on the part of the one uttering it, but where does it leave God? As for the remark itself,—it is not over-intelligent. It declares in effect that one can love God so completely as not to care whether one has an opportunity to love him forever or not. Which is about as if I should say that I love my friend so deeply that I do not care whether I ever see him again or not. All this stands on about the same intellectual level as those utterances which tell us that a desire to live beyond this existence is selfish. Suppose a man desired to live on for the sake of unselfish service?

I leave it all with the thought of the God revealed in Christ. Assuming such a God, it seems to me that we have to hold fast to human immortality to preserve the Christ-revelation of God. If we have not a God Christlike in moral qualities our reflections about immortality will not be worth much.

A few minor questions arise. One objector asks, if men mean so much to God, how could He have let ages upon ages pass before He created them. We do not know,—but we do know that that is altogether a different matter from calling men into existence and then jerking the cup of life from their lips just as they have begun to sip its sweetness. Another protests that fatherhood may not be the highest characterization of God. Perhaps not, but what is higher? Remember that we are speaking of fatherhood at its best,—not the fatherhood which gives children a start till they can go by themselves, and then lets them go, with diminishing interest in them. President Eliot once spoke a profound truth when he declared that in a true family sons and daughters grow more interesting to parents as the years pass. Still other critics will have it that we have not told what an eternal life would be like. Heaven itself forbid that we should make the attempt, for heaven would inevitably be caricatured by any of our imaginings. We do hazard one suggestion, however. Suppose we think of a state in which all human evils,—selfishness, envy, insincerity,—are done away. All manner of problems might remain to tax human resource to the utmost,—but with every ground for suspicion removed, what human energies would be released! Suppose we could have a stage of existence in which every man's yea would be yea and his nay, nay. That would be enough for a start. The rest we could leave to the unfolding possibilities of the human spirit working with the Divine Spirit revealed in our Lord Jesus Christ.

The Life Eternal

EDWIN DuBOSE MOUZON, D.D., LL.D.

Edwin DuBose Mouzon was born at Spartansburg, S. C., May 19th, 1869. He is one of the most eloquent and distinguished Bishops of the Methodist Church South, having recently delivered the Annual Beecher Lectures at Yale.

He was graduated from Wofford College, S. C., in 1889 and this same year entered the Texas Conference, his first pastorate being at Bryan, Texas. He was elected a bishop in his church in May 1910 and since then has been sent by his church to Mexico and South America to visit and administer the Missionary work in these places.

He had a prominent part in founding the Southern Methodist University in Dallas, Texas, and was Chairman of the Commission on Unification of American Methodism. He is a thirty-second-degree Mason.

He is the author of several widely read books including, *Does God Care? Fundamentals of Methodism,*

The Programme of Jesus (Cole Lectures), *The Missionary Evangel,* (Fondren Lectures) and *Preaching With Authortiy*, the Yale lectures of the past year.

The Life Eternal

By EDWIN D. MOUZON, METHODIST EPISCOPAL CHURCH SOUTH

"And this is life eternal, that they should know thee the only true God, and him whom thou didst send, even Jesus Christ."
—JOHN XVII: 3

THE Christian doctrine of life eternal finds its ground and source in Jesus Christ. It is built upon Christ and springs from him—from what he was, and what he taught, and what he did, and what he still does in the world.

It is remarkable that in all lands and in all centuries men have believed that the soul outlasts death, and in some form lives beyond the grave. And the more we think of it the more remarkable does this seem. Among various peoples, separated by race and language and distances which they have never passed, the belief in immortality is found. There were no contacts whereby the belief, having originated among one highly privileged people, might have passed over to another. Moreover, faith in immortality does not seem to be an article in a creed that could be handed down by tradition. It is more than that. It seems to be an original insight of every people and indeed of every individual. As a matter of fact, the conscious-

177

ness that I am now alive carries along with it the feeling that I shall live forever. In spite of the universal fact of death we persist in believing that we shall not die. Against hope we still believe in hope.

But at best this hope was vague and misty before Jesus came, just as still it remains a hazy belief among non-Christian peoples and just as it is wanting in power to move men mightily when arrived at only as a corollary to a reasoned theistic faith. Beyond doubt, we do find satisfaction in the philosophical arguments for life beyond the grave. But this faith has been clear and distinct and powerful only in the Christian religion. With Christ and after Christ, immortality became something other and more than the hope and fear of the masses or the philosophic faith of men like the mighty Plato. It came to be the inspiration and passion and the dominating conviction of tentmakers and tradespeople and slaves and fishermen and publicans.

Faith in some sort of everlasting continuance of the soul seems, indeed, to have been present from the very beginning among the ancient Hebrews. But there was little joy in their faith. One of the psalmists sighs:

> For in death there is no remembrance of thee:
> In Sheol who shall give thee thanks.

Here and there were certain men of daring faith who felt sure of victory over the grave, as the writer of the Sixteenth Psalm:

> For thou wilt not leave my soul in Sheol:
> Neither wilt thou suffer thy holy one to see corruption.

178

But in spite of occasional utterance of victorious faith, the fact remains that belief in immortality had little in it to inspire and transform until Jesus came, the Lord of Life and Death. In his light do we see light.

It was sunrise in the spiritual history of our race when Jesus came. "I am the light of the world," said he, "he that followeth me shall not walk in darkness, but shall have the light of life." With Jesus came a great floodtide out of the Infinite pouring in upon our world, and every river was full to overflowing and even the little streams were out of their banks. There was never another such time in human history. It was springtime in the history of faith. Everywhere flowers were in bloom and the wood resounded with the music of singing birds. In the presence of Jesus life was at the full. "I came that they might have life, and that they might have it more abundantly." Among the early disciples eternal life was a present experience and faith in immortality was gloriously triumphant. The fifteenth chapter of First Corinthians comes to a conclusion with these exultant words:

"O death, where is thy sting? O grave, where is thy victory? . . . Thanks be to God, which giveth us the victory through our Lord Jesus Christ. Therefore, my beloved brethren, be ye stedfast, unmoveable, always abounding in the work of the Lord, forasmuch as ye know that your labour is not in vain in the Lord."

Let us see just how this triumphant faith took its rise.

And first there came Jesus himself.

As St. Paul says, "He brought life and immortality to light." In all the history of the world no one was ever so thoroughly alive as was Jesus. "In him was life; and the life was the light of men." Said he, "I am the way and the truth and the life." We talk much about our kinship to Jesus. But what most impresses one is the immeasurable distance between us and him. We are but broken arcs; he is the full circle. We have brief moments of inspiration; in him the Spirit of God dwelt continually and fully. There are times when we feel that there is essential unreality about this world of sense and things that presses in upon us every day; he lived so close to the border of the other world that it was inevitable that an experience such as took place on the Mount of Transfiguration should be his. He made on his disciples the permanent impression that he was a visitor from another sphere. Before their very eyes he lived the life eternal. In his own person and in his daily way of living he bore victorious witness to the abiding reality of the spiritual. The impression he made on the men who had fellowship with him from the first finds perfect expression in the language of the First Epistle of John: "That which was from the beginning, that which we have heard, that which we have seen with our eyes, that which we beheld, and our hands handled, concerning the Word of life (and the life was manifested, and we have seen, and bear witness, and declare unto you the life, the eternal life, which was with the Father, and was manifested unto us)." The "eternal life" that he lived here in this world did not have its origin in this world nor its ending here. It belongs not to time but to eternity. He came from God and went to God. To borrow an illustration: "One evening you find among the reeds of your lake an unknown bird, whose broad breast and powerful pinions are not meant for this inland scene. It is resting midway between two oceans and by tomorrow will be gone. Does not that bird prove the ocean it left, does it not prove the ocean whither it has flown? 'Jesus, knowing . . . that He came from God and went to God,' is the Revelation and Confirmation of Ageless Life."

We believe in the life eternal because, as a matter of historic fact, the life eternal has been manifested to men. Jesus lived the life eternal.

And Jesus talked about life all the time. He at no time talked about death.

To be more accurate, Jesus did once speak of death. He said to his disciples, "Lazarus is dead." The report of Lazarus' sickness had come to Jesus. Then a little later Jesus said, "Our friend Lazarus is fallen asleep; but I go, that I may awake him out of sleep." He had carefully avoided the word "death." Rather he used the word "asleep." It was only because the disciples did not understand, that Jesus said, "Lazarus is dead." Jesus preferred the word "asleep"; for sleep means rest and recuperation and a waking-up in the morning. When Jesus had come to the sorrowing sisters, he spoke out of the fullness of life that was his and said, "I am the resurrection and the life: he that

181

believeth on me, though he die, yet shall he live; and whosoever liveth and believeth on me shall never die."

Jesus was as sure of immortality as he was of God. His fellowship with the Father was forever unbroken. His consciousness of God was a deep, underlying reality. And just so with his certainty touching the life eternal; it underlay all his teaching because it was with him an abiding and all-controlling experience. The Eternal World was his native country.

We need not now recall the many things Jesus had to say about immortality. It will be enough to mention two memorable sayings. When the Sadducees who were skeptics concerning the doctrine of immortality came to Jesus with their stock-puzzle touching the much-married woman, as to whose wife she would be in the other world, Jesus answered, "Is it not for this cause that ye err, that ye know not the scriptures, nor the power of God? . . . But as touching the dead, that they are raised; have ye not read in the book of Moses, in the place concerning the Bush, how God spake unto him, saying, I am the God of Abraham, and the God of Isaac, and the God of Jacob? He is not the God of the dead, but of the living; ye do greatly err." All this is to say that the personal relationship established between God and his children outlasts time and continues into eternity. God's friends are his forever. Therefore, Abraham, Isaac, and Jacob are not dead but alive.

The other reference is to the great words found in the fourteenth chapter of the Gospel according to John, "the dearest words that ever rang their sweet peal across the centuries"—"Let not your heart be troubled: believe in God, believe also in me. In my Father's house are many mansions: if it were not so, I would have told you; for I go to prepare a place for you. And if I go and prepare a place for you, I come again, and will receive you unto myself; that where I am, there ye may be also. And whither I go, ye know the way." There are not many words in this great saying. Details are not entered into; nothing is said to satisfy the imagination. But there is everything here to satisfy the heart. The saints' immortal hope is not a fond fiction. Jesus would never have permitted his friends to hug a delusion to their breasts. "If it were not so" he would have told us. In the "Father's house" there is room, abundant room; there are "many mansions." And whatever else may be there, Christ himself is there—"Where I am, there shall ye be also." The fellowship begun with him on earth shall be continued forever. That hope fills the heart with wistful longings, but for the time being we rest in this:

> My knowledge of that life is small;
> The eye of faith is dim.
> It is enough that Christ knows all;
> And I shall be with him.

And this marvelous thing happened: Christ rose from the dead.

I am not now venturing to say what would have happened to Christianity if Christ had not risen from the dead. For to me that is unthinkable. It was impossible that he should die and lie forever in the grave. For he was the fullness of life and he spoke only of life. It was natural and inevitable that he should rise from the dead. And he did rise.

Adolph Harnack, whose philosophy of the universe will not permit him to believe in the miraculous, nevertheless writes as follows: "Whatever may have happened at the grave and in the matter of the appearances, one thing is certain: *This grave was the birthplace of the indestructible belief that death is vanquished, and there is a life eternal.*" He then goes on to say: "Wherever, despite all the weight of nature, there is a strong faith in the infinite value of the soul; wherever death has lost its terrors; wherever the sufferings of the present are measured against a future of glory, this feeling of life is bound up with the conviction that Jesus Christ has passed through death, that God has awakened him and raised him to life and glory." Beyond a doubt, Harnack is right in what he says in these strong words. But to my mind it is a queer freak of the human intellect that it is able freely to admit a miracle in the spiritual realm, while at the same time refusing to allow a miracle in the physical world, forgetting utterly that if the reign of law stands in the way of the supernatural in the physical world it must do so also in the spiritual. For the spiritual is as truly subject to law as is the material. And after all, why try to cut the universe in two? To admit all that Harnack admits is to allow free room for the action of the living God in His entire universe. But I did not mean to argue the point: I meant only to affirm the fact. Beyond a doubt, Christ rose again from the dead. The Church is built on that fact.

The importance of belief in immortality to the early Church is seen clearly in the large place it fills in the Apostles' Creed—"I believe in the resurrection of the body and the life everlasting." And this strong faith rests on this mighty fact—Christ rose again from the dead after he had been "crucified, dead, and buried." And we shall not stumble over the simple faith that found expression in such words as *carnis resurrectionem*. What the great creed affirmed was belief in life beyond the grave in all the fullness and perfection of human personality, not a shadowy existence such as Greeks and Hebrews had thought of; but life actual and real and satisfying such as the life of Jesus had been with his disciples during the forty wonderful days. It is exactly this that we affirm when we say, "I believe in the resurrection of the body"; namely, "I believe in the persistence in the eternal world of the human soul in its entirety; I believe that the personality in its totality shall live forever with God."

And let it be kept in mind that Christianity is an experienced religion, that the great truths of our faith are truths made real in the actual experience of Christian men.

The facts of experience are the facts that count And the realities of our religion are tried out in the daily lives of the followers of Jesus. This is what keeps the faith alive and vigorous after all these centuries and in spite of all the doubters. The best of Christians in all lands and in all ages have testified that they had personal experience of the Living Christ. "This is life eternal, that they should know thee the only true God, and him whom thou didst send, even Jesus Christ." Eternal life is in an experience of Christ; to know Jesus Christ is eternal life. And it is a fact of history that holy souls have continued to know Jesus although long ago the clouds hid him from the sight of the multitude. Standing midway between "the days of his flesh" and the present time was Bernard of Clairvaux with his tender testimony:

> Jesus, the very thought of thee
>   With sweetness fills the breast;
> But sweeter far thy face to see,
>   And in thy presence rest.
>
> O Hope of every contrite heart,
>   O Joy of all the meek,
> To those who ask, how kind thou art!
>   How good to those who seek!
>
> But what to those who find? Ah, this
>   Nor tongue nor pen can show:
> The love of Jesus, what it is,
>   None but his lovers know.

And at the present hour there are millions who bear witness to the same satisfying experience of the Christ who lived and died and is alive forevermore.

186

And this experience bears fruitage in quality of character. Eternal life signifies much more than mere length of days; it means above all else quality of life. We have seen that the incarnate Christ was the revelation of the life eternal. None so fair as Jesus ever walked the earth. There was about him a celestial atmosphere. His very presence among men bore witness of the spiritual world that was his home, and whence he came. And something of the same quality of life is seen in those who have come under the influence of Jesus and whose lives are spent in communion with him. St. Paul speaks of our having the "earnest of the Spirit." Already there has been given to us an advance payment, or shall we say a pledge, of that immortality which is to be ours. As the gentle south breezes tell of the coming summer; as the flowers that cover the peach and the apple trees tell of the fruit that is presently to appear, so the quality of life that is seen now blossoming in God's children tells of the full fruitage that is to come later in the fair fields of Paradise.

It is frequently said that immortality is a doctrine that cannot be demonstrated. Well, the very same thing can be said about the existence of God. And all will depend upon what one means by the word "demonstrate." Let it be fully understood then and gladly affirmed that our main reliance both for our faith in God and for our belief in immortality is not upon philosophy, but upon experience. God does prove Himself overwhelmingly to the Christian experience. So much so that for religion men will suffer and endure and do what they will never permit or undertake for anything else whatsoever. And to the man who lives like an immortal, immortality is self-evident. The universe backs the Christian experience. Victorious and other-worldly living is the demonstration of the hope of immortality. Meantime the Christian journeys onward to God's shining City, singing as he goes:

> And this I do find:
> We two are so joined,
> He'll not dwell in glory
> And leave me behind.

The Immortal Life

JOSEPH FORT NEWTON, DD., LL.D., Litt.D.

Joseph Fort Newton has, for many years, been the editor of just such a collection of sermons as the one on which we are engaged. He was born in Decatur, Texas, July 24th, 1876, graduating from the Hardy Institute in Texas and the Baptist Theological Seminary in Louisville, Ky.

He was ordained to the Baptist ministry in 1893 and was pastor of the First Baptist Church in Paris, Texas, from 1897 to 1898. He first attracted national and international attention when he was a pastor of the Liberal Christian Church in Cedar Rapids, Iowa, from 1908 to 1916, because he was called from this comparatively unknown midwestern church to the famous City Temple, London, during war days. Here he served with great distinction during the most difficult period of all English and church history. He came from the City Temple, London, to The Church of the Divine Paternity in New York City, where he served from 1919 to 1925, when he was called to The Memorial Church of St. Paul, Overbrook, Philadelphia.

He has distinguished himself in

several fields, the first, of course, being the preaching ministry itself, in which field he is looked up to by his professional brothers of all denominations as one of the greatest mystical preachers of this generation. He has also distinguished himself in the field of Masonic literature, being the author of several Masonic books. He was at one time Grand Chaplain of the Grand Lodge of Iowa. He is the associate editor of *The Christian Century* and the author of a large library of sermons and books dealing with biography and literature.

The Immortal Life

By JOSEPH FORT NEWTON, MEMORIAL CHURCH OF ST. PAUL, OVERBROOK, PHILADELPHIA

"Jesus said unto her, I am the Resurrection, and the Life; he that believeth in me, though he were dead, yet shall he live; and whosoever liveth and believeth in me shall never die. Believest thou this?"
                                                        —JOHN XI:25, 26

AGAIN the tide of Eternity, by men called Time, has brought us to the day of all days the best, the crest and crown of the Christian Year: the Day of Eternal Life. The sweet order of Easter Day is blended with a beautiful confusion, in which the mysteries of religion are mixed with the mysteries of nature; and that is as it should be, because it is the day of the Cosmic Christ—the mighty Lord of Life and Death and all that lies between and beyond.

Out of a red sunset an Oriental poet once saw a friend riding over the desert toward his tent, wrapped in glory like a heavenly halo, and the poet exclaimed, "Glory to the Almighty, the sun has risen in the West!" Out of the crimson sunset on Good Friday, its horror and its heroism, the Risen Christ comes riding in majesty today, the best Friend of the human heart, and we cry out, "Glory to the Almighty, the sun has risen in the West!"

IF I HAD ONLY ONE SERMON TO PREACH

Out of death comes Life; out of agony comes joy; out of defeat, victory; out of sunset, dawn. Where we had least hope of sunrise, "the Son of Righteousness arises with healing in His wings," in fulfillment of his own tremendous words:

I am the Resurrection, and the Life: he that believeth in me, though he were dead, yet shall he live; and whosoever liveth and believeth in me, shall never die. Believest thou this?

How often, alas, we have heard those words as a part of the Office of the Burial of the Dead; and it was so I first heard them as a tiny lad when my father was buried. Clinging to the hand of my little mother, on that snowy day I looked for the first time into an open grave, and it seemed that everything was lost—as if the bottom had dropped out of life. Then the kindly old country preacher began the service: "I am the Resurrection, and the Life,"—never shall I forget the thrill of those words! It was as if a great, gentle Hand, stronger than the hand of man and more tender than the hand of woman, had been put forth from the Unseen to help and heal—from that day to this I have loved Jesus to distraction! Forty-six years later I stood on the same spot, when the little mother whose hand I held in days that come not back was laid away; and again the words, "I am the Resurrection, and the Life," spoke to me out of the depth of death—nay, out of the heart of God!—and there was sunrise in the west!

Of all expositions of those words the noblest is the picture, by Browning, of the death of St. John the Evangelist of Love, the last of the glorious company of the Apostles, and the only one to die a natural death. The little knot of disciples stood round watching the great head sinking lower and yet lower, until at last the flame of life flickered, and, as it seemed, went out. Loneliness, like a cold, crawling sea-mist, filled their hearts, for there was no one left who had seen the face of Jesus; no one who could say, "I heard his voice,"—and how much had been left untold! Desperately the little group tried to coax back a tiny spark of life, but in vain, till a lad ran for a copy of the Gospel, found the page, and read, "I am the Resurrection, and the Life." Hearing the Voice of his Lord, the seemingly dead man sat up and poured out his soul in one last luminous talk.

What stupendous words, "I am the Resurrection, and the Life," and how utterly empty and unreal, if not wildly insane, upon the lips of the gentle, winsome humanitarian Christ who, however heroic and fascinating, is only one of ourselves—purer, braver, more unearthly—yet guessing at the riddle of life as we have to do, knowing nothing certainly of his own destiny or ours, himself a victim of muddy, all-devouring Death, which seems to divide divinity with God. No! No! Here speaks the Master of Life and Death, the Lord of worlds other than this orb of dust, the Revealer of the meaning of life, a Voice out of the heart of things—a Voice not simply of comfort, but of command. Here shines a Light that never was on sea or land, fairer than the prophet-vision, brighter than the poet-dream. Nevertheless, this Being who towers so far above us is still so close to our humanity, his whole life so entwined with our piteous, passionate, and pathetic life on earth, that we somehow feel that what is true of him is in some degree true, potentially, of ourselves. How these two truths can be united may be hard to know—save in a paradox profounder than thought—but they are equally vivid, equally valid, and equally blessed in our historic Christian faith; and to lose either truth is to lose the other. Here, to say it once more, is the highest reach of holiness in man answered by a Voice older than the earth and deeper than death:

Before Abraham was, I am—life endless at both ends, moving with a higher rhythm, stretching away into unfathomable depths and distances; one vast Life that lives and cannot die, gathering all our broken lights into its eternal radiance.

I am the Light of the World—the sun is up; shadows of death and dark fatality flee away; blind thoughts we know not nor can name are forgotten like fear in the night. It is daybreak; life everywhere is radiant—earth is a valley with a lark-song over it.

I am the Way—the path marked out for the soul; the way without which there is no going, to lose which is to wander in a wilderness, or end in a blind alley; the Way which, if we follow it faithfully, shineth more and more unto the perfect day.

I am the Truth—the truth about life and death, which breaks through language and escapes; the truth that makes all other truth true; nay, more, the Truth that can never be uttered, but must be acted, incarnated; the truth that sets life to music.

I am the Life—the Life that interprets life; no mere story of life, but Life itself intense, creative, palpitating, prophetic; life in a new dimension, with a new radiance, overflowing, sweeping dim death away as in a flood of light and power and joy.

I am the Good Shepherd—the Shepherd of ages and journeying generations, whose heart aches with compassion for the multitudes who wander afar, seeking without finding; the mighty Shepherd in whose bosom the lambs find a haven and a home.

I am the Door—the Door out of night into dawn; the Door into Another Room in the House not made with hands, "our dwelling place in all generations"; the sheltering home of all souls, however far-wandering, where we shall see "that one Face" and be satisfied. "Behold, I have set before you an open door, and no man can shut it."

I am the Resurrection, and the Life—death is abolished, as the radio abolishes distance; it no longer exists, save as a cloud-shadow wandering across the human valley. "Let not your heart be troubled, neither let it be afraid,"—death is other than we think or fear.

Behold, I am alive for evermore—the word of One who has death behind him, never to face it again—a thing left below, defeated and outsped—having passed through its shadow, making a path of light "which shineth more and more unto the perfect day."

Now, consider. No one else has ever spoken such words to humanity; no one can do it. Never once does Jesus say, "I believe," as we must needs do, praying help for our unbelief. No. "I *am* the Resurrection and the Life,"—it is not merely an anthem of affirmation; it is a revelation of another order, rhythm and cadence of life. He does not argue; he unveils the truth. He does not promise immortality in some dim, far time beyond; he illumines it, bringing both "life and immortality to light." It is not only a prophecy but a possession—such a reversal of faith, such a transvaluation of values as baffles thought and bewilders imagination. "I *am* the Resurrection": God is here, Eternity is now, Death is nothing to the soul— it is a staggering truth, so vast that our minds seem unable to grasp and hold it. Once we do grasp it, once we do lay it to heart and know its power, then we know the meaning of the words, "Behold, I make all things new." Life everyway is infinite; the sky begins at the top of the ground. O my soul, remember, consider, and rejoice in God thy Saviour!

Here is the song of the immortal life, breaking in upon our broken days and years, gathering our fugitive and fragmentary lives into its sovereign harmony, if we have ears to hear and hearts to heed and understand. Slowly, upon our dim eyes, blinded by dusty death, there dawns the vision of a Spiritual Order

196

in which all the holy things of life—its higher values, its haunting prophecies—have their source, sanction, security, and satisfaction. To the reality of that realm all the noblest creative life of humanity bears witness —dimly or clearly—and from it the purest souls of the race have drawn inward sustaining. Of that Order "the Lord of all Good Life" was and is a citizen; its laws were revealed in his life; its meaning spoke in his words—pitched not in the past nor in the future, but in "the mystic tense";—its light became incandescent in his personality. By its serene power he was Master of disease, discord, and dark fatality— nay, more, of Life and Time and Death; in its fellowship he still lives and serves humanity, a thousand times more alive than in the days of his flesh. By the Power of Spirit his swift and gentle years moved with the lilt of a lyric, and even the tragedy of his death— in which he faced the worst and found the best— became the epic of the life everlasting.

As Dante said, Jesus taught us "how to make our lives eternal," and if we learn his secret we shall know neither fret nor fear. In prayer, in glad obedience, in high adventure—giving all, daring all—he drew the fullness of God into his life, fulfilling what others had dreamed. By the wonder of his personality he released a new power in human life—"the power of an endless life,"—power over sin, over sorrow, over brute matter and black despair. Here lies the secret of social stability and nobility, no less than of tri-

umphant character. Half a life ago Dostoievsky fore-
told the orgy of modern Russia—anarchy running mad
and running red—when, in *The Possessed*, one of his
characters cries out, prophetically:

> Listen, I've reckoned them all up: a teacher who laughs with
> children at their God is on our side. The juries who acquit
> every criminal are ours. Among officials and literary men we
> have lots, lots, and they don't know it themselves. Do you
> know how many we shall catch with little, ready-made ideas?
> The Russian God has already been vanquished by cheap vodka.
> The peasants are drunk, the churches are empty. Oh, this
> generation has only to grow up. Ah, what a pity there is no
> proletariat. But there will be, there will be; we are going
> that way.

What happened in Russia will happen among us,
when we let the altar fires of our fathers go out and
our faith fail. All the dear interests and institutions
of humanity have their basis in the eternal life, else
they cannot abide. Our human world is kept in place
and urged along its orbit by unseen forces. Thence
come those impulses to progress, those insights and
aspirations, which impel man to vaster issues—they
are the pressure upon him of the endless life. Liberty,
justice, love, truth are things of the eternal life, without which customs are cobwebs and laws are ropes of
sand. Toward the end of his life Dostoievsky divided
the race into two classes, those who know the eternal
life and those who do not, and the fate of civilization, he said, will rest with those who are citizens of
eternity. The power of an endless life is thus the

creative and constructive force of humanity, and when it is lost society becomes a pig-sty.

Here, no less, is the secret of spiritual character and personality, the two loveliest flowers grown in these short days of sun and frost. Only recently a great physician said that subconscious health cannot be obtained in one who has lost faith in immortality. Without it the noblest powers of the soul are inhibited, its finest instincts are frustrated, having no happy release and no promise of fulfillment. When we know the Eternal Life, all doors are open and the great aspirations of the heart take wings. The impingement of Eternity upon us gives to the moral sense an august authority, and makes religion not a dogma, but an Eternal Communion. Life everywhere grows in dignity, meaning, worth and grace when it is lived in the fellowship of eternal things. The Power of an Endless Life—it is the life of faith, of love, of fellowship, of joy. It makes a man stand up like a tower, foursquare to all the winds of the world, a defense to the weak or the weary. It is one with all dear friendships, with every tender tie which unites us with those nearest to us, with every bond of sympathy binding us to humanity—aye, with those whom we have loved and lost awhile.

What life really is, what it prophesies, what it may actually become even here on earth—transfiguring all "our fleshly dress with bright shoots of everlastingness" —is shown us in the life of Jesus; by the truth he taught, and still more by his personality. He was so aglow with the power and joy of life, so in tune with its vivid, creative urge and insight, that his words seem to have a life of their own, and grow. He was a spiritual biologist who thought of religion in terms of life —not of life in terms of religion—and he hardly used the word death at all; since death is not an event but a tendency, and true life is the death of death. By his death Jesus gave life to his religion, and by his resurrection he made religion a life, even the Eternal Life in Time, free, radiant, abundant, creative, victorious— a quest, a conquest, a consecration.

In literature there is an exalted zone of song wherein if a man step his footfall echoes forever, defying time and change and death: and thus the echo of an hour of prayer among the Judean hills, or a lyric sung at a Greek festival, becomes a part of the eternal speech of mankind. Just so, there is in the life of the spirit a level of loyalty, of luminous lucidity, of immaculate perception, of all-giving love, which joins the mortal to the immortal, and death is seen to be only the shadow of life as it spreads its wings for flight; only a dark room in which life changes its robe and marches on. Others enter that realm, briefly, in rare hours of insight and understanding, when the mood is pure and the vision is clear; but Jesus lived in it, obeyed its laws, unveiled its reality, and revealed its emancipating truth. Hence the strange, searching, haunting, healing quality of his words, which seem like birds let loose from a region above our reach of which we are dimly aware, and toward which both wisdom and faith point. Hence, too, the refrain that echoes through his teaching: "He that hath ears to hear, let him hear."

From that radiant realm, in the rhythm of its profound and transcendent experience of God, Jesus spoke the words, *I am the Resurrection, and the Life*. Such words are notes in an eternal world-song, a Divine Symphony which began when the morning stars sang together over a new-born earth, and which runs through all things. It is the Song of Life itself, underflowing all the tumult and tragedy of time, upbearing the life and death of humanity—its sins and woes, its griefs and heartaches—and lifting all at last into the rhythm and cadence of an Eternal Life: an august undertone prophetic of a final harmony of all things with God. All |religions, all philosophies are but broken echoes of one everlasting music, prose versions of a Divine Poetry singing even "in the mud and scum of things,"—an all-sustaining, undefeatable melody:

> It singeth low in every heart,
> We hear it each and all.

At last, rising above all discord and seeming defeat, it will break in triumphant anthems of adoration upon the throne of God, proclaiming that "life is ever lord of death and love can never lose its own." Believest thou this?

By the same token, if we would know the power of an endless life, defeating death and dull dismay, it must be by contact and fellowship with the Lord of Life. Ever the path lies at our feet, if we follow on to realize the life that is triumphant, and the road mounts steadily: "And this is life eternal, to know thee the only true God, and Jesus Christ, whom thou hast sent." For thou, O God, art Life, Thou art Reality, and Thou art our Father.

> Safe in the care of heavenly powers,
> The good we dreamed but might not do,
> Lost beauty magically new,
> Shall spring as surely as the flowers
> When, 'mid the sobbing of the rain,
> The heart of April beats again.
>
> Celestial spirit that doth roll
> The heart's sepulchral stone away,
> Be this our resurrection day,
> The singing Easter of the Soul:
> O gentle Master of the Wise,
> Teach me to say, "I will arise!"

The Pressure of Immortality

FREDERICK WILLIAM NOR-WOOD, D.D.

Frederick William Norwood, a minister of three continents, having started his brilliant career in Australia, being well known and popular as a preacher in the United States, and finally having attained a maximum amount of success in the great White Pulpit of The City Temple in London, is one of the best known preachers in the English speaking world.

He graduated from Ormond College, Melbourne, Australia and received the honorary degree of D.D. from Oberlin College, Ohio, and from Ursinus College, Ursinus, Pennsylvania. He has been the minister of churches at Canterbury, Brunswick, North Adelaide, and was an Honorary Captain of Australian Forces in the World War.

He is not only a most popular preacher before American audiences, but his books are also well known to American readers as well as to

English and Australian readers. Some of his books are *The Cross and the Garden, Sunshine and Wattle-gold, Mood of the Soul, The Gospel of the Larger World.*

The Pressure of Immortality

By F. W. Norwood, City Temple, London

"How are the dead raised up? and with what body do they come?"
—I COR. XV: 35

IF I had but one sermon to preach, and its theme had been fixed as Immortality, I should choose as text these words of Paul's, but I should alter the punctuation marks. Instead of two notes of interrogation I should insert two notes of exclamation! Instead of asking incredulously or timidly "in what way" or "by what means are the dead raised?" I should want to cry out in amazement at a fact which few appear to observe, that the raising of the dead and their reappearance in new bodies are the most common of all phenomena.

When the news of the death of Jonathan was brought to David, he exclaimed, "How are the mighty fallen!" That was not a question. It would be absurd to treat it as such. He was not wanting to know by what particular instrumentality Jonathan had fallen; it was an exclamation of amazement, "How are the mighty fallen!"

In like manner I should want to cry out, using Paul's words but not his punctuation, not asking captious questions but exclaiming in surprise: "How are the dead raised! With what body do they come!" How insistent is the pressure of immortality upon us mortals!

I should not be doing wicked violence to Paul, for of course these words are not strictly speaking his own at all; they are merely the questions of some hypothetical person, drawn in by the hair of his head for the sake of argument: "Some man will say, 'How are the dead raised? With what body do they come?'" What Paul thought of that man is indicated by his next words, "Thou fool!" I need have little ceremony for this lay figure, this devil's advocate, this blockhead. I rather appreciate Paul's temporary departure from politeness. There are times when it is justified, and I think it is justified not merely in the case of incredulous, sceptical people, but also, alas, in the case of very good and sincere people such as preachers and scientists who presume to tell us, reasoning from analogy, either how the dead are raised or else how they cannot possibly be raised.

It would be quite right if some one said to any one of us at such times, Thou fool! What else is he who has an ocean of talk and but a thimbleful of knowledge?

And yet I am sure that humanity is not left confronted with an insoluble enigma. The correct attitude of man towards this problem is not one of timid questioning. Of course if we mean, by what means are the dead raised, or in what manner are they raised, we have to confess our ignorance. But that is not so very unique in life. We should not believe in many things if we refused to believe except where we had dissolved away the last film of impenetrable mystery.

The tail of the question mark is rooted deep down in the abyss. We discover the sequence in which things happen, and in our loose way we say we know "how" they occur merely because we know the order in which they occur. Every man's final mental decision is a venture of faith. The denial of the sceptic is as likely to be an act of faith as the credo of the believer.

We are guided through life by a recurrence of phenomena so unvaryingly repeated that we accept it without further question. "Probability," as Bishop Butler used to say, "is the guide of life."

I say there is nothing that we know more certainly than that the dead are being raised, and evermore appearing in new bodies. If you will look I will show you "ten thousand times ten thousand and thousands of thousands" of corroborating phenomena. Surely it is some obscuration of vision that makes Death seem to us like the inscrutable Sphinx. It has its own brooding secret as everybody knows, but it is a secret that is more than half divulged by every flower that lodges in some chink in its colossal frame and every bird that pausing for a moment perches upon its gloomy brow.

A great part of the reason for our mental distress upon this question is that we never think of it except when our hearts are sore. We only ask about immortality when Death with his baton has commanded the missing of a few beats in the chorus of life. When we preachers preach about it we do it in an atmosphere of sorrow. Our very phrases are portentously solemn, from the midst of which a stray smile would slink away like a convicted trespasser. This very chapter from Paul which is in far too happy a vein to be an apologetic, we only read at gravesides, where grief is too stony eyed to see, or too conventional to feel.

I am sure no one will misunderstand me if I seem to be callous concerning our common human woes. I just ask you to consider that the emergence of the dead in ever-changing bodies is the most ordinary thing in the world. Re-embodiment, reincarnation, resurrection, call it what you will, is so familiar that if ever we do discuss the matter when we have passed over the silent river the angels may smilingly say, "Look back and see. All the way you have been walking amidst myriads of manifestations of the very thing you were so constantly questioning."

Look at nature. There is not a flower that blooms, nor a tree that lifts high its leafy stem nor a bird that cleaves the air nor a creature that inhabits the forests or plains that has not left behind it a long trail of so-called death reaching back and back and back to a distance so remote that the mind sinks before its contemplation; yet every living thing at this moment is the million-fold embodiment of a reincarnation.

The man is surely morbid who goes out over the fresh yielding turf, stooping over the flowers, lifting his eyes to the trees, listening to the whirr of wings and the voices of field and woodland and can see and hear nothing but death.

Where is this death? Can you find it? How many dead flowers have there been? How many dead trees? How many dead birds and creatures have cumbered the soil? Where are they? Can you find them? You may find them at the moment when some plant or some creature has lately made the act of renunciation, but where is all this death? Is it not a living world? Has not this thing we call death reissued in life, and has not the very essence of it been dissolved into invisible potency wherewith the veins of life are perpetually throbbing?

It is not a dead world, it is a living world, and every living thing seems to exclaim, How are the dead raised! Indefinite reincarnation is the only explanation of this teeming world we are inhabiting today.

I am amazed at my own embodiment. Before I could stand here with this "one sermon" I am to preach, there had to eventuate millions and millions of renewals of life, reincarnations, resurrections. They lie behind me somewhere in the invisible, stretching back and back and back I know not how far.

I saw an article in a popular journal the other day, one of those snappy clever articles which constitute too much of our mental pabulum. I failed to retain it so I can only refer to it by an indistinct effort of memory, but it made the assertion that there is not a person living today who, if he traced back his ancestors to the days of Queen Elizabeth, both his direct and collateral ancestors, would not find he was the representative of millions of people. Every single person is in himself an epitome of a myriad resurrections wherein the dead being raised have clothed themselves with new bodies.

It is happening all the time. I do not suppose for a moment that I am the first preacher in the line that produced me. I seem to see some ancestor, skin-clad and belonging to the Stone Age of whom I am a partial re-embodiment, with striking enough physical and mental resemblances which even the centuries have not obliterated. In our family, so far as I can learn, the effort to produce preachers has been incessant. They keep on reappearing, never in the same, but always in a different body. I feel the latest results ought to have been much more satisfactory.

How are the dead raised! With what body do they come! Of course I know what will be said of this. You will say that we are still in the realm of the physical. There has been actual contact between these ancestors of ours, the intercommunication of a material life-fluid. But in death life seems to stagger down into a cul-de-sac.

A hundred years ago very few people thought far back into the past. They supposed that the earth was only some six thousand years old but they had great faith in the eternal future.

To what a past eternity we have now surrendered. The sturdiest materialist never ceases to tell us that we can trace our traits and characteristics back to the prehistoric jungle. We have loaded eternity upon our heels and taken it off our wings! But one way or another it seems as if eternity is "set in our heart."

Now I do not dispute the necessary connection of the physical but it does not seem to me to endanger the validity of the spiritual. Men live again and yet again in the works of their hands. I should think the greatest man who ever lived, judged upon the material plane, was the man who first invented the wheel. Nobody will ever find out who he was; no doubt it was not one man but a number of men. Somewhere there must have been a man who first made the amazing discovery that one could do marvelous things with a sledge if one could construct a circular disc with a rod through its center. If that man could look now upon the innumerable adaptations of his thought, and see how this thing that came to him with glad surprise in those early primitive days is now the most marvelous mechanical feature in our modern be-wheeled world how amazed he would be at its ever-recurring, ever-varying re-embodiment. After all, the power that created the wheel was mind-stuff, soul-stuff. Something dwelt within that man, however primitive he may have been, that never was in any other creature less than man.

I admit that the Almighty uses material means for the re-embodiment of life, for the reincarnation of thought and of truth and of ideas. But I cannot persuade myself that all I have received from the past is physical. Anybody will agree that there cannot be one particle in our bodies which belonged to us, say seven years ago, and yet I think almost certainly we are repeating in our thoughts and in our characters things that were in our ancestors before the name of our nation was ever upon men's lips. I feel perfectly sure there is not a physical particle in my frame that was of my mother's body when she first held me in her arms and kissed me, and yet I know there is a lot of my mother in me! I cannot persuade myself that it is only by physical means that God works His miracle of resurrection, rejuvenation, reincarnation, call it what you will. It grows upon my soul with amazing wonder that this thing we are always asking questions about is just the thing that is beating in upon us like the waves of a limitless sea. It is not a new thing at all, it is of the very stuff and texture of life.

Man lives again and again in the contrivances that his hands fashion, but after all the best kind of influence is too subtle to be called physical. This old city in which we dwell is not inhabited alone by its present day population. They are the least important portion of the vast fraternity that gave this city its character. Late comers we are. We have just hurried in through a mysterious door that shrouded the past and in a little while we shall be passing out of another door that hides the future. We have not done much for our city yet. What have we done? Built a warehouse perhaps, done a little thing here or a little bit there.

THE PRESSURE OF IMMORTALITY

I have come into this pulpit for a few short days which in a generation or two will seem no more in length than the time occupied by the passing of a band in the street. I have said a few things but I have not done much. They have done it! they whom we call dead!

Mostly I have been reading the words of the dead from this old Book. Mostly I have been recapturing the thoughts of the dead. Mostly I have been telling over and over again the pathos and the adventure, the hopes and the fears of the dead, and just because I have done that with some verisimilitude, I suppose I have found some echo in the lives of the living. Take away from me the influence of those you call dead, and I am nothing but a leaf, driven by the wind.

Dead? It is the dead who live! With what body do they come? Watch the progress of truth all down the centuries. See how men have snatched up a torch and run with it a little way before they fell; see how another and yet another has carried it on still farther, how the old ideas have been again and again re-embodied. "How are the dead raised! With what body do they come!"

The higher we climb in the scale of life the more subtle, the more spiritual and the more eternal are the influences that find perpetual re-embodiment. There is nothing so immortal as truth. There is nothing so endlessly repeated as life.

The most we need admit in the presence of death is that we have lost sight of the material nexus. A

213

many sided personality has subsided into silence. There seems nought left but the memory of it and some vague thing we call his influence. We suppose that will lessen as we forget him. But is it necessarily so? There is an infinity of influence in the world the origin of which has been forgotten. Not the famous but the forgotten and the unknown are the real arbiters of destiny. I repeat it is the dead who sway us much more than the living. And as for the great and famous dead, will any say they live less than when they were the tenants of the flesh? Is Shakespeare less or more than when he reached the height of his social ambition in Stratford-on-Avon?

There is another Name one almost shrinks from mentioning as a mere example in an argument—but did Christ die on Calvary or did he enter into life? Was the Incarnation a terminal point or has he not been reincarnated innumerable times in the hearts of the lowly? It is a world that is peopled and not alone by those who are in the flesh. Of course for most of us today, indeed for all of us, life is not lived on the scale of the infinite but on the scale of the finite. It is one little plot of earth that we live upon and our boundaries are not far away. We love and we lose. We have our dead and we sorrow over them. But we know how they still live, how they are raised, and with what body they come. It is not just memory; it is more than that. How many things they say to us now that they never actually said when they were with us. There are many people to whom the dead

214

are more important than the living. They do not talk much about such communings because others do not see what they see and feel what they feel, but they have their own private gardens in which they walk in renewed fellowship with those who have risen from the dead, they reappear to them in bodies which are at once familiar and yet new.

These things no one can deny. The marvel is that we do not see them in perspective. But once seen we know that we ought not to be content with a timid question upon our lips but to exclaim with genuine wonder in our hearts, "How are the dead raised!" "With what body do they come!"

The pressure of reincarnation upon us is amazing. The reappearance of the dead in new bodies is the most common of all phenomena.

But we have to confess that we have lost track of the physical nexus which alone to many of us seems to guarantee survival after death. Could we but find the soul as our fathers thought must be possible even were it in the pineal gland as they supposed, or were it anywhere else, how comforted we should be.

We are so pathetically mere mechanicians. We never doubt the mystery of the birth of a baby because not alone is it a fact of experience, but because we can localise a tiny drop of fluid, a microscopic ovum. Heaven knows they seem inadequate enough to account for all that follows,—growth, constant change and yet persistence of type, but we are satisfied because we are mere mechanics. And we suppose that even the Almighty can do nothing without mechanical appliances.

Yet we must know that everywhere there is something over and above that for which physics can account. The most thorough-going materialist has never yet accounted for his own actual thought which surely means that he has not really accounted for anything.

When you have catalogued all the impediments of life you have still to begin to explain life itself.

It is life for which death is a mere anticlimax. A rational world at least must not end in a trivial conclusion. Is it possible to deny immortality and still believe in a reasonable world? I do not mean in a law-controlled conditioned world but in a totality which has made adequate use of its materials. A world that leaves the worms rioting in high carnival and can give no account of the intellectual, moral and spiritual qualities it has so recklessly expended is, to say the least of it, vastly inferior to its own offal. It has made garbage of all that alone gave it dignity.

This ever-labouring effort to reincarnate life which throbs through every vein of the world from the amoeba upwards would have reached its gehenna of repulsiveness if it left Jesus Christ in the whole meaning of him to fatten worms! Before the significance of a possibility like that the whole universe must come to judgment at the bar of reason. Were it true, no decent man could respect the world or the fate that sent him to live in it.

THE PRESSURE OF IMMORTALITY

There is but one thing which forbids us to write futility over our frustrate purposes and our cut-off days; it is life so long and so expanding that Love may finally be all in all.

Through all the ascending cycles of life nature persists in raising the dead and clothing them in new bodies and at the apex of experience, stimulated by these witnesses but believing beyond the letter of their evidence, a reasonable man would say with Jesus, "God is not the God of the dead, but of the living!"

Had I but one sermon to preach upon immortality I would not let it trail off into the inane question of an apprentice mechanic, "How are the dead raised?" I would close it with a ringing exclamation, "How are the dead raised! See with what new bodies they do come!"

It is the everlasting motif which in Christ becomes vibrant, personal, compelling. Its significance in him is not quantitative but qualitative. I believe in the Life Everlasting.

Sorrow the Way to Immortal Life

CARDINAL WILLIAM HENRY O'CONNELL

His Eminence, Cardinal William Henry O'Connell, was born in Lowell, Mass., Dec. 8th, 1859, receiving his A.B. at Boston College in 1881, graduating from the North American College in Rome, Italy, June 8th, 1884, being ordained a Priest in the same year in Rome.

His first public recognition was his appointment as Rector of the North American College in Rome, Nov. 21st, 1895. Two years later, June 9th, he was named domestic prelate, and appointed as Bishop of Portland, Maine, in 1901.

In January of 1905 he was named Assistant at the Pontifical Throne, and special envoy of the Pope to Japan in 1905. He was named Archbishop of Constance and coadjutor with Succession of Boston in March of 1906, succeeding to the See of Boston on the death of Archbishop Williams in August of 1907, being elevated to the Cardinalate Nov. 27th, 1911.

Cardinal O'Connell is the author of more than a dozen volumes of sermons, addresses and proclamations to his people, and is called upon in Boston to represent his great church on all public occasions.

Sorrow the Way to Immortal Life

By His Eminence William Cardinal O'Connell,
Archbishop of Boston, Massachusetts

"Behold! this child is set to be a sign that shall be contradicted, and
a sword shall pierce thine own soul."

—LUKE II: 34

IN CELEBRATING the feast of the Seven Dolors of our
Blessed Lady, how strange it seems that she who
was destined by the Eternal Father to rise to the
highest place of honor among His creatures should be
also the one who, after Himself, should taste the bit-
terest fruits of sorrow, and drain with Him that cup
even to the very dregs. How strange that she whom
we honor by the great title of Mother of God, should
be also styled by us Mother of Sorrows. Yet so it is.
Side by side with the picture which represents Mary
enthroned amid the angels of God's court, is that other
piteous sight which the Church unveils for us today,
the Mater Dolorosa of Calvary. She stands alone in
the gathering darkness. The sun refuses to lend his
light to the awful spectacle; thick clouds gather in the
heavens that make a gloom horrible and appalling. An
awful silence reigns, broken only by the sobbing of
those beneath the Cross.

221

Even the strongest bend their heads and avert their eyes from the heart-rending spectacle. Not so His Mother. Weak and broken-hearted, spent and wasted with grief she may be, but there at the foot of the Cross she stands, with face uplifted to that of her Son, that His last gaze may rest upon her; that He may see at least that she understands it all; that she is resigned to it all, and that she is the true Mother even to the end. Let us still look at her and learn from her. Her heart beats as if it would break. A well of sorrow rises to her eyes; the tears flow unheeded down her pale cheeks, but not a moan escapes her. She only repeats the words she uttered to the Angel when he announced to her her great honor at the annunciation: "Let it be done to me according to Thy will." Who can look upon that sight and remain hardened? Who can gaze upon that Mother and not weep? Who can see this sinless Virgin, this holiest of women, standing there bereft of the only love of her pure heart, of the sweet solace of her life, of the honor of her age, standing there gazing steadfastly upon the fast-closing eyes of her Son, as the death pallor spreads across His features, as the eyes grow dim and Jesus dies,—her Jesus, her God, her Son, her All.

Yet it is not simply to move us to compassion; it is not simply to make us weep that this picture of the Mother of Sorrows is held up to us today. However much we might sympathize with Mary's grief, if we stopped there our sympathy would be poor indeed. From the foot of the Cross she speaks to all the world,

"—I am the Mother of Sorrows. Let all who mourn come to me, the chief of mourners, and let them learn that in the midst of suffering God is nearest; and that if we but keep our faith and eyes fixed upon Him, our sorrow will be but a stepping stone to eternal joy."

Let us then contemplate this scene today with liveliest faith; and side by side with Mary at the foot of the Cross, let us try to understand seriously the place that pain, sorrow, and grief have in the make-up of our human lives.

Wherever we look in the world we behold suffering. We need no great argument to prove the truth of this statement. The history of human nature, our knowledge of the world about us, our knowledge of our own experience teaches us that this is a truth beyond any possibility of doubt.

Some there are who go upon their way rejoicing in the sunshine of life, plucking the flowers as they pass. The air for them is filled with the song of birds, and every breeze comes to them laden with fragrance. Day after day goes by repeating the same pleasant experience. We look at them and in the healthy bloom of their faces, in the joy that glistens visibly in their eyes, we read the happiness which as yet alone has been their lot. But alas! Who does not know that soon, very soon, all this must change? Some cloud will arise to cast a sudden gloom across this sunlit path. A loving relative, or still dearer friend has gone never to return; and then the roses go from the lip and cheek and the joyous light from the eyes, and life is never again what it was before. The bitter sting of pain has left its trace.

Some there are who from their earliest years are shut out from every human joy. Perhaps disease fastens early upon the poor victim, and year after year rolls in, each one bringing with it only another burden of pain and grief. Dire poverty may come, even in the very morning of life, to wither with its touch the simple joys of childhood. But whether it be by an occasional sting or by continuous pain that it makes its presence felt, one thing is sure, sooner or later, grief, sorrow, suffering must come to all—to the king, to the poorest peasant and beggar alike. How true, alas! is that text, with which we are all but too sadly familiar—"Man born of a woman, hath but a short time to live, and is full of many miseries."

Suffering is a reality. It is something that happens to all the world, and therefore to us. If hitherto it has not crossed our individual path it is only deferred. But the chances are that to every single soul here present sorrow has come in one form or another, and we know, we are sure, that it must come again and again even till we stand upon the edge of the grave, even until at last we lay down the weary burden of our lives, and pass to judgment. A fact faces us which we must meet and from which there is no escape. We sometimes feel impelled to cry out, Why, oh why is this? Was I born but to suffer? Did I come into the world only to weep and groan with burdens? Is life at best then a torture? Have I been created only to meet disappointment and poverty, or sickness and pain? or bereavement, or disgrace, or dishonor? Why am I doomed to all this? Why should life be but a place of anguish? Is God merciful who allows all this? Is he my Father who can see me thus afflicted?

Let the atheist answer. Let him explain if he can the presence of suffering. Let the philosopher answer, and explain why human life is so full of misery. They cannot. They must both shake their heads and reply that it is fate. Religion alone is ready to respond— the Christian religion—the religion of the Crucified, of the Son of the Mother of Sorrows! Pleasure, joy, prosperity are treated and discussed in the learned books of the infidel. But of the use, the benefit, the necessity of misery, wretchedness, adversity, Christianity alone is eloquent. She alone knows their origin; she alone has the secret of their mission; she alone knows that though they be called evils, by men, they are often blessings from the loving hands of a merciful God, favors from the bountiful heart of a kind Father to enrich and ennoble and elevate those who in prosperity might forget the true end of life and the fact that "here we have no continuing city, but seek one to come."

Oh, yes, the infidel can understand the suicide who, too cowardly to face misfortune, ends life with a bullet; but only the Christian can understand the heroism of the man who seeing naught before him but adversity and sorrow, still manfully refuses to turn his back upon it but meets it calmly, content to stand on his guard till his Master calls and his General sounds the signal for retreat.

It was Christ alone who taught the true office of pain; it is only his religion that understands the true value of suffering.

By pain and adversity, God chastens and purifies the soul. He sends us grief that He may make us think less of the world and more of Him. He sends us sorrow, to weaken the hold of sense, and strengthen the power of the Spirit. It is as necessary as the bitter medicine to the sick child, as the surgical operation to the diseased frame. As the mother who loves her child best will administer the bitter draught, or hold with her own hands the struggling arms of her son while the surgeon applies the lancet, even though all the time her own heart is tortured; so the Eternal Father Himself grieves for the necessity which compels Him to send us pain and sorrow in order to make us think of what we are, to make us realize for what we were created.

How often have we seen God's natural blessings, health, wealth, physical strength, personal beauty— things in themselves good and desirable—perverted to all manner of evil, operating to the destruction of the soul. It is too often the experience of life. In prosperity we see things in a false light, we think always of ourselves. We forget God; we run after the baubles that fortune holds out to us; we forget the real treasures which are above. But pain dispels the dream. It wakes us with its sharp pang to the reality. From being almost gods, as we think we are, we fall to our proper place, as miserable, dependent creatures, whose very breath and existence is the free gift of the Creator.

Yes, sorrow, grief, pain, beget humility before God, and humility is the first step to eternal salvation.

Naturally, pain, sorrow, ill-success are hard to bear while they last, but when they are gone, when the misery and grief have passed, they leave behind them the bright sunshine of God's grace and pleasure in the soul, which compensates it a thousand times for all that it has undergone. It is St. Paul's teaching: "Now all chastisement for the present indeed seemeth not to bring with it joy but sorrow; but afterwards it will yield to them that are exercised by it, the most peaceable fruit of justice."

This is the true effect of sorrow, it sets us free from earth, lifts us up to heaven and unites us even to God. Oh wonderful mystery! Oh incomprehensible economy! This is the lesson of the Crucified, this is His message from the Cross. This too is the secret of Mary's strength, that makes her so like her Divine Son. Through Cross and Passion to the Resurrection: through pain to eternal joy; through suffering to everlasting peace. Alas, for the man who does not grasp these sacred truths.

This is what our holy religion teaches: Manfully to bear the burden that is sent to us in whatever form it comes, knowing that it is meant to bring us nearer to God, and to draw us farther away from evil. What though we do not see how it is to accomplish this. We never know our nature as God knows it. We never shall know how many men have been saved forever by patient bearing of life's ills for God's sake. We never can know how many have been eternally lost by refusing to recognize behind the rod that chastens the loving hand of our Heavenly Father.

Some Saints there have been in God's Holy Church who realized so well the dangers of prosperity that they have prayed for sorrow and adversity. St. Ignatius prayed that his order of the Society of Jesus might always be persecuted, and St. Teresa used to cry out in the midst of her agony, "More, God, still more! Let me suffer, not die!"

We cannot hope to aspire to such perfection. If we can but school ourselves to be calm in adversity, to be patient in suffering, to bear the ills and stings of life with a noble Christian equanimity we shall have learned the Christian's lesson of the Mater Dolorosa. Our nature shudders at the sight of grief. But what we can do is to teach our poor nature to bear it all for God. To make our own the prayer of Christ in the midst of his awful Agony, "Father, if it be possible let this chalice pass from me. Nevertheless, not my will but Thine be done." We are not called upon to seek disappointment, dishonor, sickness, poverty, and want; God has raised up His Saints to give the sublime example of such heroic virtue. But we are daily called upon, and must be ever called upon, while we live here below, to meet all misfortunes, when they come to us, with Christian fortitude; not to rebel against the hand that sends them; not to do as Job's wife advised him, "curse God and die"; but in sickness as in health, in adversity as in prosperity, in pain as in joy to look up in the midst of our grief to God. It may be hard to bear it; we may have to look through blinding tears up to the Cross as Mary did. But the faith that is in our hearts, our confidence and hope in God will help us to stand as Mary did. Weak and sore and grieved our nature may be, but inwardly we shall find Peace; for not all the pain of illness, nor the bitter pangs of loss or bereavement can rob us of our trust in God, who chasteneth whom He loveth, "and scourgeth every son whom He received"; so that after the bitter ills of earth are at an end He may lead them into the Paradise of Eternal Joy where there is "no more death; neither sorrow, nor crying; neither shall there be any more pain; for the former things are passed away."

Five Facts for Failing Faith

DANIEL ALFRED POLING,
D.D., Litt.D., LL.D.

Daniel Alfred Poling is better known to his host of friends all over the United States as "Dan" Poling than by his more formal name or degrees.

He was born in Portland, Oregon, Nov. 30th, 1884, and graduated from Dallas College in Oregon in 1904. Taking his A.M. in 1906, he has continued his student life in Ohio State University and Columbia.

He is known widely for his life of service in several fields. First, he is a preacher and a great one, now being pastor of the Marble Collegiate Church on Fifth Avenue in New York City. Second he has been for years President of the Christian Endeavor Society of the United States and is now the editor of *The Christian Herald* of New York City, besides carrying on a great radio service for young people every Sunday afternoon in a National hook-up which reaches all over the nation.

Not content with these wide fields of service, Dr. Poling has written several books a year, including books of sermons, devotional books, two novels, and two war books, all of which have a wide reading, particularly among young people. He served

for a year as special war-work speaker
under the Y. M. C. A. and was
at one time Prohibition candidate for
Governor of Ohio.

One of the youngest ministers in
the United States to have occupied
so many important positions in the
church world, he has time to give
himself in consultation to thousands
of young people through his prolific
correspondence in response to his
radio addresses. He is one of the
younger group of ministers whom
we are glad to have represented in
this series on Immortality.

Five Facts for Failing Faith

By DAN POLING, NEW YORK CITY

"Now faith is the substance of things hoped for, the evidence of things not seen."

—HEBREWS XI: I

WEBSTER gives us a definition of "fact": "anything strictly true; a reality; also sometimes applied to even general and abstract truth." Our subject—"Five Facts for Failing Faith," implies that there is such a thing as faith; implies at once the fact of faith, which no man will deny; and also implies that faith may fail. Faith in God, faith in man, and faith in one's self. Faith in faith itself may fail!

A greater tragedy cannot be imagined than the failure of faith. No other failure is absolute. Men rise from business crashes to achieve even greater success than they knew before financial calamity overtook them. One plan proven faulty results in another being tried, which succeeds. Nations pass from triumph to bondage, but emerge at last from slavery to reach positions of political distinction far beyond their previous stations. Truth crushed to earth will rise again—will rise again upon the hands of faith. But when faith fails, the captain of industry surrenders; acknowledges himself beaten; retires from the field.

233

When faith fails, there is no other plan. When faith fails, nations go not into temporary eclipse, but perish. When faith fails, truth, sore beset, sinks in her wounds without defenders, and the soul puts out his own eyes.

Faith is defined by Webster as a "firm conviction of the truth." Theologically, faith is the assent of the mind to the truth of what God has revealed; "a hearty reliance upon God and His promise of salvation through Jesus Christ." When faith fails here, death becomes a haunting terror, and life remains not worth the living. "Faith is the substance of things hoped for, the evidence of things not seen" is Paul's sublime definition. "Substance of things hoped for"—an inspired paradox. Faith and substance; mind and matter; spirit and material. And a fact again and again demonstrated, we have found it to be, that without faith substance fails and the material disappears.

Does our subject also imply that the times in which we live are times of failing faith? Well, for some, I fear for many, they are. Within the week I have talked with a woman who bears high recommendations from institutions in a foreign country. Particularly competent she has been when entrusted with children. But, as the result of an accident, she no longer has the old confidence with which she once went about her profession. When she is invited, even urged, to fill the position she has been fully trained to fill, and in which she has had wide experience on two continents, she trembles from head to foot, and becomes practically helpless. At the moment she is working as a

234

domestic under hard circumstances when in her own field there are many unfilled positions. Lacking faith in herself, the substance of her learning, the material of her training, avail little. And often mental, and even physical misfortunes are responsible for a spiritual collapse that leaves a once imperial life shorn of its authority. "He can, because he thinks he can"— is tremendously true.

Years ago a young attorney came to the minister of a great city parish and said, "Doctor, I have lost my faith. Can you help me? More than anything else I need it now. I have already a measure of success, and the future is full of promise, but I have lost my faith. I lost it somewhere here among the books and questions of men and universities. Doctor, I must have it, or all will be lost. Can you help me?" And again and again the story of the young attorney is being duplicated in this highly organized, hurrying, questioning day.

Young people are particularly involved. The advanced study, once entered upon by a limited number, now engages practically all youth, or influences them through popular, however superficial, magazine and periodical discussion. Sharp distinctions are made between conservative and radical thinkers in all groups of society—economic, social, political and religious. Too often, these distinctions, which actually involve only minor matters, are lifted into the prominence of major events. Young people are bewildered by the involved and acrimonious debates of their elders.

What to mature minds may be little more than an intellectual diversion, becomes to minds less mature, cause for doubt, and sometimes the invitation to denial. Youth is naturally the age of faith. When youth becomes cynical, the event has a particularly tragic significance.

The world needs today what another has called the "unreasoning enthusiasm of youthful devotees"; needs this ardor and abandon to sweep away the suspicion and cruelty and denial of the years. Let us then, we who hold the high places of scholarship and moral authority, think not so much of ourselves and those with whom we match our theories—rather less of ourselves and of these and more of our sons and daughters.

One evening I found myself face to face with a young Ohio collegian, the president of his class, and an officer of the college Y.M.C.A. He was terribly unsettled. A distinguished leader of religious thought had challenged his sense of fair play; had, as he keenly felt, insulted his intelligence. He came to me saying, "If that man is right, then I am not a Christian." Almost he was ready to renounce his faith. The wrong attitude on my part would have completed a moral catastrophe. God gave me the intuition of his true status, and the answer for the question of his soul.

Again and again with others in a similar crisis that Ohio experience has helped me to be measurably helpful. "Whether you are a Christian or not depends upon no man but yourself; yourself, sir, yourself with Jesus Christ," I said to him. "The man may be right, or the man may be wrong. You should worry about him. Jesus said—'*Come, follow me.* I am the way, the truth and the life,' and as for knowing whether you are in that way or not, Paul's standard has never been surpassed. 'The fruit of the Spirit is love, joy, peace, longsuffering, gentleness, goodness, faith, meekness, temperance: against these there is no law'; with that high command of Jesus—'Love thy neighbor as thyself.' "

The Christian life is not a matter of definition, right or wrong; intellectual affirmation right or wrong; scriptural interpretation right or wrong. The Christian life is an experience in, with and through Jesus Christ. Give youth a reasonable chance, a sympathetic opportunity—give youth your confidence, and youth will emerge from the fog of uncertainty and superficiality, the twilight of doubt, aye, and the darkness of denial that we, youth's elders, are too often responsible for.

There was a time in my life when, had a man said to me of those principles which in my soul are now supreme, those articles of Christian faith which are now dearer to me than life itself—when, had any man said to me, "*These you must believe,*" I would have replied, "*Then I am not a Christian.*" It was the Isaiah spirit of "Let us reason together"—it was the "Come and see" invitation of Jesus himself that brought me through the darkness into the marvelous light and liberty of sonship.

This, then, is the background for the message of the

hour, and for all who find faith failing there are five restoring facts.

First, the fact of man. Whatever man is, he is. The temptation is strong to exalt him; to see him through the eyes of a worshiper; to see him at his best —the conqueror of continents, the master of the ocean and of pestilence, shaper of racial destinies—to see man struggling and overcoming. But it is not this view of man that strengthens my faith particularly. It is rather man the hopelessly inadequate; man the fallen creature of the Godlike race. One of the first discoveries made by the infant is the discovery of human limitations. Your baby is forever reaching for something just beyond him and howling at the top of his lungs with chagrin and disappointment over his failure.

There are many pictures of man—in some he rides at the head of victorious armies, or stands upon frontiers of physical and scientific discovery. In others he riots with the strength of youth, plays with love and beauty, courts the muses, lolls upon couches of voluptuous ease. There are pictures of sin, and there are pictures of sacrifice, truth, error, shame and glory but the picture truer than any other is this picture of his babyhood, where his arms are too short to bring him to his heart's desire. There are times, sir, when this fact of man's inadequacy drives one nearly mad. Your dearest treasure lies with breath half throttled in his throat and turns appealing eyes upon your burning, anguished face; or your son comes with the fresh terror of some disgrace to plead for relief from the shame; or debt closes slowly in upon you, grinds away your freshness, leaves you flimsy and threadbare like the old coat on the broken man; or disease strikes you down and you feel its remorseless, wasting progress.

I stood one afternoon in the spring of 1913, and watched the rising waters of the Scioto river eat through the embankments that keep it from the homes of West Columbus. I saw steel rails snap like pencils of slate, and a bulwark thrown up to last a century, falter and disappear like sand. Then houses crumpled like cardboard, and spread out like thick cream upon the waters, and men and women and children bobbed about in the maelstrom like fisherman's corks—men could not save them. And yet, sir, the final checking up after that experience, revealed a rising tide of faith. As the river subsided and returned to its course; as the people buried their dead, and sought for their silt-covered property lines, they turned their eyes outward and upward, and their voices lifted again the cry—"My help cometh from Thee," "Our help is in the name of the Lord who made heaven and earth." Always in such times of man's inadequacy, faith strengthens.

Faith strengthens in such a time because of the tremendous fact that companions man's inadequacy—*the fact of God*—God who is adequate. A sister church in America has been discussing a rather unusual question—"What is God?" Such a study cannot be without great profit. And when all other qualities and attributes of God have been considered, the adequacy of God might well be selected as all-inclusive—omnipotent, omniscient, omnipresent—adequate; adequate for man the inadequate. Adequate for us all in all things.

We reach out to take possession of life's dearest prize and find ourselves still with the shortened arms of childhood. We stand by and watch the floods of adversity sweep over the things of our heart's desire. We feel the creeping palsy of the years, the withering blight of adversity. In our extremity, we cry— "Whither shall we flee?" and in our extremity lies God's opportunity, and He answers, "My grace, my grace is sufficient for you. Come unto me." He knows, and knowing understands. He is present and ready to help. He is able and places Himself at our disposal. Our God is sufficient.

"Yes, ah, yes," I hear you say, "but God is your assumption, not necessarily a fact." Not necessarily a fact? Let us see. Above the great concourse of the Grand Central Station is a tiny engine and several obsolete coaches, forerunners of our twentieth century giant Moguls of the rails. What does that tiny engine prove? Many things, to be sure, but chiefly this —the fact of an engine maker; the fact of an engine maker who knew the genius of his creation, who was its master, who was its creator, who was sufficient.

The most sublime fact of human life is the fact of personality; the fact of you. *You*, not your eyes and hands and voice, but *you*. That which we miss when you are gone—gone though for a little while we still may touch your hands and caress your face. Reason leads me to God. Behind every visible manifestation is cause, and at the beginning is First Cause. First Cause would satisfy me were I dealing alone with continents and oceans, stars and planets; aye, and bleating flocks and the winged creatures of the air. But you baffle me until reason rises to another level and I see *"in the beginning God,"* God who is the greater. God who is the Creator, to be sure, but God who must be Personality; Personality omniscient, omnipresent, omnipotent.

These are facts for failing faith. The fact of man —man the inadequate; and God—the fact of God,— the adequate.

A third fact for failing faith is the fact of Death— the universal fact of death. Death which Horace declared is "the ultimate boundary of human matters," death which comes equally to us all and which makes us all equal when it comes.

> The Prince who kept the world in awe,
> The Judge whose dictate fixed the law;
> The rich, the poor, the great, the small,
> All levelled; death confounds them all.

There is no arguing against the fact of death—for, as Bryant says in "Thanatopsis,"

> All that tread
> The globe are but a handful to the tribes
> That slumber in its bosom.—Take the wings
> Of morning, pierce the Barcan wilderness,

Or lose thyself in the continuous woods
Where rolls the Oregon, and hears no sound,
Save his own dashings—yet the dead are there:
And millions in those solitudes, since first
The flight of years began, have laid them down
In their last sleep . . .

And now on Long Island the man who wrote exquisite lines sleeps with the millions of death's solitude.

But what is Death? One has written:

'Tis slumber to the weary;
'Tis rest to the forlorn;
'Tis shelter to the dreary;
'Tis peace amid the storm;
'Tis the entrance to our home,
'Tis the passage to that God
Who bids His children come
When this weary course is trod.

Such is death—Yes, such is death.

But no poetic passage can remove the natural antipathy that the normal man has for death. It is quite unnatural to welcome death. The philosophy that cultivates such an attitude in men and women is neither human nor Christian. God created man to live and not to die, and God's will for us all is that we should live well and long—as long as we can and as well as we can by His grace. But with so personal and so appalling a fact as death; appalling, I mean, by mere human and natural conception—with so appalling a fact as death, so constantly crowding up to us

—what is there in this fact that strengthens failing faith? What is there in this fact, I say—"The knell, the shroud, the mattock, and the grave, the deep damp vault, the darkness and the worm." What is there in this fact that strengthens faith?

The first instinct of a human being under attack is to defend himself. He looks for a weapon, or a means of protection. Eventually he plans a campaign of defense. Man regards death as his greatest natural enemy, and fights against him with every resource of his mind and will. And yet after all the æons of time that have elapsed since God set the forces of life in motion, man has discovered only one way to conquer death—only one way—not by the waters of a magic spring; not by the curative powers of a mysterious drug; not at last by the husbanding of strength, the conserving of physical resources; but *by loving beyond it. By loving beyond death* we conquer death. Because man instinctively loves beyond death, irresistibly loves beyond death, death strengthens faith.

Let the stark and naked arms lift a darling baby from its cradle and weeping eyes lift then to the unfailing hills whence cometh their strength. Strike down the strong man in his prime and his friends find their consolation in "I am the resurrection and the life." Invade the sacred precincts of a home; break up with unexpected blow the happy family; leave tears for laughter there, and above the weeping you will hear the song of rapture.

Glad I am to know the crossing,
In the sullen tide between;
Hither banks that fade and tarnish
And the fields of living green.

Tear a brother from the side of a self-styled infidel and the infidel will turn from blatant denial to cry— "But in the night of death, hope sees a star, and listening love can hear the rustle of a wing." Faith baffled becomes faith strengthened. It is in death, in the stern, cold, unrelenting fact of it that I have seen the fires of hope rekindled and felt again the immortal flame that shineth more and more unto the perfect day. Death strengthens faith because instinctively, irresistibly, omnipotently, we love beyond it.

My most convincing human reason for belief in immortality is personality. Personality already referred to, but joined now to life's fulfillment. Nothing is ever annihilated. No form of life ever dies without some form of resurrection. The oak has its acorn and for every sunset there is a sunrise. Forms may change but life itself moves with a tide as irresistible as the recurring seasons. My reason tells me to apply the principle in all of this to personality. Personality may change its residence and lay aside the flesh that clothed it, but never is destroyed.

And for me the immortality of personality involves future recognition, recognition beyond that which we call death. Accepting personality as I do, future recognition is inevitable, for recognition is a fundamental part and quality of personality. Personality is you.

Recognition distinguishes you from me and each of us from all others. Yes, my convincing human reason is personality and with it goes future recognition. Logically, personality, in whatever form or manner, must survive and with personality must go recognition.

Yes, death, the fact of death strengthens faith. With the fact of death walks, hand in hand, the fact of life. Twin sisters dark and fair they move together in the souls of men.

Without opportunity for a doubt, life is a fact. "What Life Is" has been the subject for many a wise debate and learned dissertation, and will continue thus to serve so long as life itself shall survive. But the fact of life is at the very beginning of wisdom. Why then do men question—"What Is Life"? Why? Because no man has yet satisfactorily answered the question. Because no man has ever explained life. Because no man knows what life is. Reason has yet to solve life's riddle. Science has yet to explain life's reason. Not until you are able to reduce God to the component parts of a laboratory demonstration will this problem be completed. Perhaps it has never occurred to you that life which we cannot explain, but which unmistakably is, we must accept by faith. Inevitably life, until you deliberately, finally deny it—until you destroy it, strengthens faith. What a theme!

And what is it about life particularly that strengthens faith? The beauty of it? Verdant, flowered, well-watered, singing nature; green in the springtime, radiant in summer, flaming in autumn, and frozen in winter. But no beauty of nature is permanent. Indeed no attribute of life save one is permanent. Beauty, strength, joy, ambition—all pass and passing leave behind their disappointment, their disillusionment, their question—What is life? But one attribute of life does not change; does not pass; does not fail— life's resurrection—life's rebirth. From acorn to tree, and back again and on forever, with God forever at the beginning, is the way of the world! I have said that reason has yet to solve life's riddle, but, sir, it is the logic of events that leads even a savage to chant songs of immortality. The desert blossoms and dies to flower again with another springtime. The humble worm sleeps through a season and then awakes in colors that match the rainbow—am I not more than these! The fact of life strengthens faith. Life which is forever renewing itself. Life which we have now and which is but as an infant's span to that glorious immortality our faith lays confident hold upon.

The fact of man; the fact of God; the fact of death; the fact of life—five facts for failing faith. Failing faith! What is this fifth fact that strengthens failing faith? Why, faith! Faith strengthens failing faith; faith that struggles with itself, but struggling grows. Faith that staggers like a drunken man, but staggering staggers on. Faith that doubts. Faith that questions. Faith that cries in mighty travail, sweating drops of blood: "I believe, I believe; help thou mine unbelief." Faith is an instinct, but it is also an exercise. Its origin is divine, but even divinity must serve to survive. Do you say, "But I cannot believe." You may say it, and you may believe it, but you are mistaken. Reverse the order! Shift from negative to positive. Rise in the morning declaring your faith and not your doubt; praying Paul's omnipotent prayer; shouting to all the winds that blow "I believe!" If you do, I pledge you my word, I give you the word of God, you will find faith mightier than denial.

Man, God, Death, Life, Faith—these five! And the five are one! They issue in life conquering death and in man forever hid with Christ in God.

The Death of Death

MERTON STACHER RICE, D.D., LL.D.

"Mert" Rice, or "Mike" Rice, as he is called in Detroit by most people, is the pastor of the largest white Methodist Church in America with a membership of over four thousand and perhaps the most perfect combination of the beautiful and the practical in church architecture ever erected in Detroit.

He was born in Ottawa, Kansas, September 5th, 1872, and graduated from Baker University, Baldwin, Kansas in 1893. He was ordained a Methodist minister in 1894 and served in several small Kansas towns before going to Duluth, Minn., in 1904 where he remained until 1913 when he was called to the North Woodward Methodist Episcopal Church. He began his ministry here but the church burned down and he continued his pastorate in an old Tabernacle for many years, when his devotion and willingness to serve in this ramshackle old church was rewarded with one of the most beautiful church edifices in America, costing over a million and a half dollars.

In addition to being a great preacher Dr. Rice has written several books in recent years which are numbered among best sellers in religious books. They are *Dust and Destiny, The Expected Church, The Advantage of a Handicap,* and a biography of William Alfred Quayle, whom he knew from boyhood, perhaps more intimately than any other human being. His book is called *William Alfred Quayle—The Skylark of Methodism.* Dr. Rice has been considered as the most outstanding material for the Bishopric of the Methodist Church for several years but has each time refused this election saying that he would rather remain in the pastorate than to be an executive officer in his church.

The Death of Death

By Merton S. Rice, Pastor Metropolitan Methodist
Church, Detroit, Michigan

"Whom God hath raised up, having loosed the pains of death:
because it was not possible that he should be holden of it."
—ACTS II:24

THIS very striking verse, selected for my text now,
is a part of the reported sermon of Peter. His
preaching was powerful. The immediate results were
overwhelming. He had a rugged challenge in the way
he said things that made always of his contention an
immediate appeal. The root reason doubtless being,
that his preparation for such preaching was founded
in convincing experience. He had swept about every
note on the gamut of experience. He was preaching
upon the import of the crucifixion and resurrection of
our Lord, to those who had in themselves a measure of
relationship to the death, that would justify him accusing them. It was so soon after the supreme tragedy,
that we cannot bring our minds to imagine, how folks
would even tolerate such criticism for what they had
done, had it not been known to be true that a resurrection of the one they had crucified had taken place.

251

How can we account for this bold preacher? He is the man who but a very few days before was fearful of being classed as even an acquaintance of this Christ. This is the slinking fellow of the darkness, who even by the taunting finger of a servant girl, pointing him out as he stood with some others warming his cold hands at a little fire, grew so cowardly as to deny, and deny, and in mad fear to deny again his Lord. But here now in daring defiance of criticism, he is challenging to serious blame, a multitude.

Hear this bold preaching. "Ye men of Israel, hear these words [of mine]: Jesus of Nazareth, a man approved of God among you by miracles and wonders and signs, which God did by him in the midst of you, as ye yourselves also know: him, being delivered by the determinate counsel and foreknowledge of God, ye have taken, and by wicked hands have crucified and slain: whom God hath raised up, having loosed the pains of death; because it was not possible that he should be holden of it. . . . This Jesus hath God raised up, whereof we are all witnesses. . . . Therefore let all the house of Israel know assuredly, that God hath made that same Jesus, whom ye have crucified, both Lord and Christ."

Thus preached the now emboldened man. The coward of yesterday, the daring challenger of today. The denier of yesterday, the very earnest preacher of today. What could have produced such a complete change in his conduct! Something must be found that will offer a reasonable explanation of this reversal. It cannot be some mere mental shifting. It is not to be accounted for by some change in theology. A whole life has been redirected.

I hail you, and greet you, my Christian friends in the faith we hold, that I am sure is the only plausible answer to the transformation of the Apostle Peter. The resurrection of Him whom they crucified will alone explain it.

I sometimes think we have become so accustomed to the conduct of our now well-settled faith, that we do not in slightest measure comprehend how essential to the Christ we know of the Gospels, is the tremendous meaning of the facts that come pouring forth from the enshrouding darkness which settled like a pall over Calvary that awful dying day. If you take away from what we hold of the life of our Lord, the fact of the resurrection, then are we left with nothing at all about this Lord of ours today, other than ordinary biography written with some chapters in somewhat involved mystery. But where is the life that can be written with every stroke of mystery erased?

We of this Christian era, however, stand possessed of a Christ who did not fade from the world in the enveloping gloom of Calvary. There must be brought forth some explanation of the Christ today. Ordinarily the burial of a character is a biographical close of his career. Either the Christ of history is a creation of the wildest imagination mankind ever knew, or else he did break through the bonds of death as the Bible declares, and establish in the convictions of those who by his death had been utterly broken and scattered, the new confidence greater than any they had ever had before they had seen him die. This great Christ of ours has made for himself too great a place in the world, from Bethlehem until now, to allow a borrowed grave to be the closing incident in his career.

Recognizing such a fact as that has of course been the prompting reason for all those who have endeavored to deny the resurrection, to refuse the Gospel story, and in its place to build them a new sort of a Christ to whom no resurrection would be an essential. The resurrection, like Phidias' name on the shield of Minerva, has been so completely interwoven into the whole story of Jesus, that you cannot take it out without destroying the whole structure. Unless Jesus Christ in his own dying actually slew death on its own ground, his death brings to a close a misspent life, and writes its finish in terms of its own inability to accomplish that toward which his whole career naturally tended, and in exploitation of which his history ever since has been triumphantly declared.

I was much interested in the thesis and treatment of a sermon preached and published by Dr. Morrison, of the *Christian Century*, which he titled, "Easter, Inevitable." It is a contention for the presumptive evidence of the great event. "He was born a man at Bethlehem. He was born the son of Man on Easter Day." It is the recognition of the place among us of what the great fact has come now to be, "made manifest of the appearing of our Saviour Jesus Christ, who hath abolished death, and hath brought life and immortality to light through the gospel." The very confirmation of the claim of the resurrection of Jesus, is Jesus himself, as we know him in the gospel record, and as he has made his conquering way on into a whole world's attention and life. "It was not possible that he should be holden of death." What words these! saturated indeed with meaning that even yet awaits their fulfilling evidence, for this Christ came forth then, and is alive now with the death of death, carrying dead death in his triumphant hands. Bringing death a trophy in his resurrected return. There was never a moment of uncertainty in his divine soul as he saw the Cross appear before him. Though to us it may even yet present conditions we cannot fathom, yet to him there was never a hesitant moment. "I lay down my life. . . . I have power to lay it down, and I have power to take it again." Thus he speaks in the very midst of whatever we dare call the gloom of Calvary surely meant to him.

It was beyond, and through, and out of all such struggling experience as came to the troubled disciples from such an inexplainable event, that Peter knelt before the death-triumphant Lord while across his tumultuous soul surged the trying memories of his own personal failures in the crucial hours. There was born the preacher of the irresistible Christ, which must be the conviction henceforth of everyone who dares proclaim this Gospel. Always and everywhere henceforth this Christ is the inevitable Lord. Having loosed the pangs of death, he comes now bringing death in his pierced hands. He comes the hero of the grave. He comes the slayer of death, King of Kings, Lord of Lords. Dead, but alive forevermore. O death, where is thy sting? O grave, where is thy victory? We have grown bold to shout our challenge before this death-bound world. Thanks, thanks, thanks be unto God who giveth us the victory through our Lord Jesus Christ. The death of death! The death of death! We raise our monument to death, buried forever behind the daylight of our risen Lord. We would build a monument of death, out of the symbolisms of life. We would brush back all the mantle of darkness that has been heretofore draped about the thought of the grave, and there instead, the immortal light of the Kingdom where the sun never goes down. We would remove all the broken columns, and quenched torches, and sealed urns, and weeping willows, that have crowded their sad and defeated symbolism into our graveyards, and in their places we would erect our new symbols of victory. Instead of broken columns, we would set erect and perfect pillars in the temple of our eternal home. The quenched torches we would kindle with a fadeless flame. The sealed urns we would open with the deathless fragrance of life forevermore. The weeping willows we would replace with the glad trees of life that grow on either side of the stream that flows out from His eternal throne. And life forevermore shall become our anthem to displace the sobbing strains of the sad miserere.

256

THE DEATH OF DEATH

There used to be a strangely powerful idea that grew more and more as the career of Napoleon spread its flaming way across all Europe. His soldiers, with an ever increasing loyalty to him, and in a sense of complete confidence, came to believe he was resistless. They carried that belief, as a contagious feeling, with them into battle. There went swelling along the long lines of the troops a strange thrill whenever the great general rode forth on his famous white horse. They called him, "The Ten Thousand." They did believe he was irresistible.

That tradition went down one most defeat-ridden day, and the final chapter of such an ill-founded human measure was written in a dark dreary story of a restless, comfortless prisoner. Yonder on a lonely island prison shore, alone, alone, alone walked the restless form of the dethroned hero. Through long weary days he walked the lonesome shores with his impotent hands clasped behind his back. At times in the sudden grip of memory, he would call out orders to his troops marshaled by his memory alone, only to be answered by the measured tread of the watchful guard. And he died, alone in a storm. Today his impressive tomb, holding the great sarcophagus in which his body lies, affords an ever attractive center of interest in Paris, back to whose confines they brought him long after death had won over him that common victory from which no mortality can escape.

That which was only a shattered tradition about Napoleon, has become a veritable fact in Jesus Christ.

257

The Captain of our Salvation rode forth to conquer, and rides now a conqueror. Death sealed Napoleon. Death was the sure plan the enemies of Christ selected as the riddance of him. If we can but kill him, said they. If we can but see him dead. Death is the end of folks. That has always been the closing note of life as we know it. I have just finished reading one of the most famous of all the recent biographies, and it ends abruptly at his bed with this, "The members of his family with handkerchiefs held to their eyes, went sobbing out of the room." That is the way we conclude human biographies.

They killed him. They tauntingly killed him. They killed him in mockery. They degraded him in death. They made roughly sure he was dead, by the thrust of a great tearing spear into his side.

He is dead! That is the end of the ordinary. No matter how very extraordinary any of these ordinary mortals may have become, death strikes them dead. There lies the great Elizabeth, the proudest and perhaps the greatest of the queens. Canon Farrar tells us in one of his chapters about Westminster, that one day a ragged, dirty, little urchin from the streets crawled with boy curiosity, down along the side of her tomb that had fallen into disrepair, and reached in his dirty little hand and laid it on the dead breast of the long departed proud queen. That is what death does for the mighty. They killed Jesus. They buried him. They sealed his grave. Then they went with determined satisfaction back to their ways. He is dead! That is the end of that.

The whole history of the Christian Church, however, is the comment on their plans. They reckoned without their reasons. They had not calculated on the loosening of the bonds of death. Crucify Him! What of it, O Cross! We call back now into the face of that infuriated mob that lifted him on that trembling hill. We shout now our defiance to those who were sure they had that day closed that story. The story of Jesus Christ does not close at a grave. Death cannot be the final chapter in the life of our Lord. Life must be the final chapter in life, and it is a continuous chapter. Had death but had hands strong enough to hold him, it would have long ere this hour have held him, in all the deadness that death can mean.

Julian, the old apostate of Rome, in the mockery of his bitter hating unbelief had a coffin made for the Nazarene. But they never put him in it. And when the trembling old hater came up to die, fear-struck and defeated utterly, he cried as terror seized his soul, "Thou hast conquered, oh Galilean!" Everything the ingenuity of Hell itself has been able to devise, has been done across the centuries to fasten a death grip on this living Christ of ours. Through it all he lives and grows in his influence and power.

Christianity as it lives today throughout the world, and as it moves steadily onward to its God-determined triumph, is not a mere abstract thing comprehended in a few formulas of belief, and framed in a lovely collection of theoretical ideals. Christianity is an omnipotent personality. Christianity is Christ, the living, inevitable Christ. Death could not hold him. He is death's conqueror.

There is irresistible power in that defiant fact today. It is felt, too, in a whole world's life. It has pushed back prejudice and hatred. It has commanded attention. It has transformed the symbol of shame, which was chosen as the crushing instrument of his death, and made of it the whole world's most impressive and universal symbol of service. It has made vile men clean. It has transformed weak men into giants. It has brought light into the world's darkness. It has sent hope singing its glad way into every discouragement. It has set a quenchless torch beside every grave, and poured divine balm upon every sorrow. It has turned triumph into a whole world's song, and wreathed every shadow with a promise, and struck death dead.

My heart is glad in my faith. I stand at the empty grave of my resurrected Lord and preach our deathless Saviour. What a welcome word for such a world as we know this world to be! Not a hidden cottage where death will not come. Not a humble tribe in the densest forest of darkest life, but death has found. Not a great mortal on the topmost crest of the highest-hung wave of civilization who can escape death there. There stands death! You, and you, and you, are stared at by it. Who can break this tyrant? Who can bring us hope? Who can set a song of victory in the human heart? Is there any voice that can be raised in all this deluge of death?

It is to answer that human plea the Christ of Easter has come. He died to answer it. He arose from the dead to answer it. He is alive forevermore to answer it.

Our faith is not troubled today. Some day, that which he himself wrought out in his own tomb, shall run triumphantly into every tomb everywhere. The omnipotent shoulder will lift every barred gate from the long-holden hinges, and the broken bonds of death will be shattered at the triumphant feet of immortality, and we from whom the hold of death shall have likewise been shaken, will unite our eternally thankful songs to acclaim him, The Almighty! King of Kings! Lord of Lords! All in All! Blessed Forever! Jesus Christ, the Lord of Life, alive forevermore!

The Things of Time and Eternity

LEYTON RICHARDS, M.A.

Leyton Richards was born March
12th in Sheffield, England. He received his early education in Sheffield,
England, in Grand Rapids, Michigan,
in Glasgow University, and Mans-
field College, Oxford.

Dr. Richards preached during his
college days in Richmond, Maine,
and after leaving college has been
minister of the Peterhead Congregational Church in Aberdeenshire;
College Street Independent Church,
Melbourne, Australia; B o w d o n
Downs Congregational Church,
Manchester; temporarily the minister of The Church of the Pilgrims,
in Brooklyn, N. Y., and Pembroke
Chapel in Liverpool. During the
war he was the Secretary of the Fellowship of Reconciliation in London.

Dr. Richards is familiar with the
United States of America, having
spent several summers here speaking

in various parts of the nation. Since
being called to the famous pulpit at
Carr's Lane Church, Birmingham,
he has especially attracted the attention of the church in America.

The Things of Time and Eternity

By LEYTON RICHARDS, PASTOR CARR'S LANE CHURCH, BIRMINGHAM, ENGLAND

"Our light affliction which is for the moment worketh for us more and more exceedingly an eternal weight of glory; while we look not at the things which are seen but at the things which are not seen; for the things which are seen are temporal, but the things which are not seen are eternal."

—II COR. IV: 17, 18

THIS affirmation by the Apostle Paul seems to justify a reproach often levelled against Christianity; which is that it is so concerned with a world to come that it is heedless concerning the needs and problems of the world that now is; or it is so intent on Eternity that Time is of no account. The reproach appears to be warranted to a still further degree if we give the Greek of the text its full value, which does not appear in any of our recognised versions of the New Testament; for the promise is not (as usually understood) that bodily affliction in every case issues in spiritual blessing but that it does so only for those who have a consciousness of eternal values. From this point of view the text may be paraphrased thus: "The passing afflictions of earth yield a glorious compensation in the world to come for those, but only for those, whose chief concern is not for the things of Time but for the

265

things of Eternity." As such the text seems to identify Christianity with what has been contemptuously called "Otherworldliness."

In recoil from this reproach therefore, modern Christians and Churchmen have been desperately anxious to prove that the world-to-be is of quite secondary importance; what matters, in other words, is not a heaven beyond the grave but heaven on earth; and so the prime interest of modern religion is not the "many mansions of God" but houses for the millions; not the blessedness of Eternity for immortal souls but happiness amid the things of Time! Yet with all the modern emphasis on "things seen and temporal," and with all our concern for the well being of men's bodies, we are all conscious that "the times are out of joint"; for there is some fundamental distemper in the world's condition in the presence of which economists and politicians and social reformers and even violent revolutionaries are as helpless as the churches are alleged to be.

It is of course obvious that if this brief "three score years and ten" is the only life there is, then our first and only task, as was seen ages ago, is to make it as comfortable as possible; and the only common sense is expressed in the familiar motto "Let us eat, drink and be merry, for tomorrow we die." But if this life in Time is but a preliminary for a larger life in Eternity, then it may well be that we have all lost our bearings by surrendering too lightly our interest in "otherworldliness." There is certainly no doubt that a concern for the hereafter is a prominent, if not the dominant, interest of the New Testament writings. For instance Jesus urged his followers to live a Christian life for the sake of "their reward in Heaven"; his frequent references to "eternal life" as the goal of existence point to the same direction; so also do his parables of judgment with their promise of heavenly bliss for the righteous. Consequently it is in full harmony with this emphasis on Eternity when Paul declares that "affliction" is of spiritual value for those whose gaze is fixed on something other than the world of time and sense. In a sentence, take "otherworldliness" out of the Christian gospel and it forthwith ceases to be the gospel of Jesus Christ.

Then what is the explanation of this frank appeal to the fact of Christian immortality, with its emphasis upon the life beyond? We shall find an answer if we consider in the light of this "otherworldliness" first certain problems of our personal life, and secondly some problems of the social order.

I

The Problems of Our Personal Life

The problems which arise in this connection are those which come from contact with our Christian faith, and it is only to these that attention is directed. The problems are seen when sorrow or struggle or suffering is viewed in the light of the Divine Providence affirmed by Jesus Christ; indeed apart from this faith in Providence there is no problem to consider, for it is only the seeming contradiction between the hardships of earth and the Love of God which constitutes a problem to be solved. Or to put it otherwise, if the universe were governed by an almighty devil the things which now distress our minds might still afflict us, but they could not raise the disturbing questions which emerge when affliction is brought into contact with our Christian faith in a divine beneficence. So it is that Christian people are perplexed whenever joy is shadowed by loss; or life overwhelmed by death; everywhere about us is the "still sad music of humanity"; and in the presence of experiences like this a Heavenly Father's providence often seems a mere fiction of the theologians. We see this when we turn to the practical activities of our Christian life; the Way of Christ often seems so futile and ineffective, a mere case of "much ado about nothing." For instance, let a man follow the way of Christian love when all the world is given to violence or hatred, and as a reward he will be brushed angrily aside! Or let him take the way of service when the world is governed by selfishness, and his reward will be to be deemed a fool and ignored! That is, Christian effort in the world as it is seems doomed to failure and futility.

It is admittedly difficult to escape such a conclusion if our experience is viewed within the limits of this world's life, where the Sin of Man thwarts and qualifies the Will of God. But if, as our Christian faith affirms, there is another world where the Will of God

268

is triumphant, and where the supreme reward of His children is to share His Life and to be in fellowship with Him and His saints, then we can regard the sorrows, the sufferings, and the defeated efforts of earthly life not as divine inflictions but as defects and handicaps imposed on a world where Man is free by his sin to defy the Divine Purpose; and yet since the Christian life is immortal, therefore to persist in the Christian way despite the handicaps of earth is to prepare the soul for an eternal glory which will far outweigh the brief tribulations of Time.

The modern mind with its concern for material values is repelled by this appeal to the future life; also it has to be admitted that such an appeal has often been stretched further than faith requires, and has been made the pretext for an unchristian acquiescence in things-as-they-are. But because "otherworldliness" has been abused that is no reason for discarding it; for the only thinkable alternative to the compensations of a future life is blank despair, the pessimism which denies the Providence of God and leaves Mankind helpless and hopeless in the grip of earthly circumstance. If therefore we would preserve our faith in God as we face the problems of our personal life, we must focus the emphasis of our being "not upon things that are seen but upon things that are not seen; for the things which are seen are temporal, but the things which are not seen are eternal."

The need for a Christian emphasis on Eternity is fairly obvious when we consider the things of our personal life; for earthly life is short—a mere three score years and ten—and we consequently need another life to complete it, and to fulfil its meaning and purpose. But this is not the case when we turn to the things of our social life; for society lives on after the individual dies, and therefore among human concerns the ordering of society seems least of all to demand care for a world beyond the grave. Yet even here things go wrong unless our chief concern is not for the things of Time, but for the things of Eternity. Let us then consider further from the standpoint of Christian "otherworldliness":

II

THE PROBLEMS OF THE SOCIAL ORDER

It seems axiomatic that economic justice, social good, and political ideals are the business of THIS world and not of the next; for they arise out of, and are directly concerned with, "things seen and temporal"; they concern matters of wealth and wages and capital, the organisation of the state, of industry, of labour, questions of production, distribution, consumption, and other aspects of our material activities. But the Christian view is that life HERE is a preparation, or an education, for life HEREAFTER; on any other terms indeed it is difficult to find a rational significance in earthly existence. It therefore follows from this that the way in which we order our economic and social and political relationships is of vital importance, not only for the world that-now-is, but also for that-which-is-to-be. It is very much like the education of children. Schooldays are entirely without meaning apart from a subsequent manhood or womanhood, and it is the requirements of adult life which determine every academic curriculum. It is the same in regard to that "eternal life" whose characteristic is a conscious fellowship with God, begun in Time and continued in Eternity. On any sane view of human destiny that Life is the thing of supreme importance; but our place or condition in that Life is of necessity determined by the way we react to THIS Life of Time and Sense; or, in other terms, our personal well being in Heaven turns upon, and is conditioned by, our social behaviour on Earth. For instance, if we are selfish HERE, how can we expect to be selfless THERE? If for us the Will of God in Jesus Christ is secondary amid the social relationships of earth, how can it ever be primary amid the spiritual relationships of Heaven? Or if here and now we fail to "love our brother whom we have seen, how shall we ever love God whom we have not seen?"

A true Christian "otherworldiness" therefore, so far from inducing indifference to earthly things, actually enhances the value of right social relationships on earth, just because such relationships find their fulfilment in the social life of heaven; and this intimate association between the social and the spiritual, the temporal and the eternal, is of the essence of a Christian approach to the problems of the social order.

271

Consequently if we would solve these problems we must first of all learn to fix our gaze "not on things seen and temporal, but on things not seen and eternal."

The value and necessity of this "otherworldliness" is seen when we consider the fact of trying to maintain human society without any lively sense of God, or any serious concern for the life to come. Look at Western civilisation as we know it today, where Christianity over large areas has lost its hold as a conscious sanction for social relationships; and however we explain it, social ethics with its eye on the things of Earth is proving no substitute for religion with its eye on the glories of Heaven. The dominant motive, for instance, in the economic world, whether we think of it in terms of capital or of labour, is not "treasure in Heaven," but what Mr. R. H. Tawney (in his *Acquisitive Society*) has called the "incentive of private gain." But note the result;—when "gain" is not in view service is withheld, men are unemployed, the world's resources are idle. Or it may be that the "incentives" clash, and then we get industrial disputes, social disturbance, and in the last issue international war. Is it a mere accident that a society which dismisses with contempt the idea of a "Hell" in the world to come should by its own irreligion produce for multitudes a veritable hell in this world of Time and Sense? Then what is the remedy? And the answer is in the Apostle's injunction that we should "look not upon things temporal but upon things eternal." So then, as with our personal problems, so with our social problems; earthly life must be regarded as a preparation for that fellowship with God which is the prime purpose of our being, and which is begun HERE and perfected HEREAFTER.

But that involves the application of a new motive to the problems of the social order; thus the modern insistence on a social gospel means generally that the function of Christianity is to create a better social order; and in such a view the test of religion is this: Can it, or does it, solve our social problems? Can it abolish slums, get rid of war, bring order out of chaos, mitigate the extremes of wealth and poverty? In a word, can it make Earth into Heaven? If not, the modern mind is inclined to dismiss religion as just so much useless lumber. But to expect religion to serve the social order is to put the cart before the horse; for if Man's fellowship with God is the supreme purpose of existence, then even the social order exists *for the sake of religion*, and not vice versa. That is, the final value of any social system is to be judged by this criterion—does it lead men to God as seen in Jesus Christ? Is it designed to make men fit for the fellowship of Heaven?

It is there that we find the Christian motive for social betterment. It is not merely a desire for economic justice, for we do not know what justice is apart from the Will of God; it is not even pity or sympathy for the poor, the oppressed, or the dispossessed; for such motives may lead us sadly astray, as anyone can testify who has experience of public charity. The Christian impulse is nothing less than a passionate desire to give a foretaste of "Heaven" to all the sons of men in this world of Time, and so equip them for the relationships of a world that is timeless and spiritual. It is this desire which involves a reordering of the world's life after the pattern of the Kingdom of Heaven. The Christian therefore will seek social justice not merely to bring equity or happiness into human life, but because in no other way can men be free to establish that fellowship—of Man with His Maker, and of Man with his Brother—by which alone the purpose of life is fulfilled. We want to abolish slums not merely because they are a blot upon modern civilisation, but because a slum—or for that matter a suburb—is a standing obstacle to our fellowship with God; so also we seek peace between the nations not merely because war is horrible and cruel and wasteful, but because the operations of war are always a denial of fellowship with God and with our Brother Man; the so-called "glory" of the battlefield is always a contradiction of the "Glory of God" in Jesus Christ. The same principle applies in every realm; that is, the aim of the Christian is not first of all to make men happy or comfortable or respectable or safe, but always to link Man's life to God's; for only on such conditions can the souls of men be trained adequately and fully for the life of Eternity and for that immortality which is the destiny of the Christian soul.

"We have here no continuing city," says the Scripture, "but we seek for one to come." It is that fact of universal experience which sooner or later compels us to take account of "the things which are not seen and eternal." And that is why the viewpoint of Jesus is so true to the facts of life; for he saw all things— the world, the men and women in it, their activities and experiences—he saw them all in their relation to the Life of God, and therefore against the background of Eternity.

The Possibility of Personal Immortality

ELWOOD ANTHONY ROWSEY D.D.

Elwood Anthony Rowsey was born at Buena Vista, Va., August 5th, 1898, and took his A. B. at Ashland, Ohio, in 1921. He did special work in Philosophy of Religion at Toledo University and received his D.D. from Oskaloosa College, Iowa, in 1924 and his B. Th. from Auburn Theological Seminary in 1928.

He was Associate General Secretary of the Ohio Christian Endeavor Union in 1920-21, and has been pastor of the First Westminster Presbyterian Church at Toledo, Ohio, since 1922. J. M. Ramsey, editor of *The Expositor,* characterized Dr. Rowsey as "Pastor of a metropolitan church, Chautauqua, Convention, Commencement speaker, world traveler, magazine writer, author of dramatic book sermons, and above all a precious friend of fellow workers."

James Schermerhorn says of him:
"Dr. Elwood Rowsey combines
southern fire vividly with northern
force, and he relates his messages to
life problems."

The Possibility of Personal Immortality

By Elwood Rowsey, Pastor, First Westminster
Presbyterian Church, Toledo, Ohio

"If a man die, shall he live again?"
—JOB XIV: 14

OUR view of immortality rests upon our general
view of the universe, and our conception of the
character and purpose of God. No section of doctrine
requires more rethinking. Much in our traditional
view is pre-Christian, Jewish and Apocalyptic.

I received a letter recently from a very brilliant professor in one of our graduate schools of theology, and
he closed his reference to immortality with this sentence: "It is not being written about in our Religious
Periodicals very much at present;—I wonder why?"

I do not attempt to answer that question, but I am
convinced that many people who formerly parroted
the traditional belief of the elders, are giving serious
though silent consideration to this subject.

Many times men and women hesitate to speak of
some of the most real experiences of their lives. An
outstanding illustration is the muteness of some of the
soldiers of the great war. Many of them who passed
through experiences indescribably horrible refrain
from relating them, even to their friends. There are

279

thousands of men and women who think as did the old minister who was approached by a young enthusiast desiring that the old minister give him all of the religious reasons for belief in immortality, that he might argue with a friend. . . . when the young man failed to get the old gentleman to talk, he burst forth with the interrogation: "Have you no religion at all?" "None to speak of," was the gentle reply.

There is a small group who would laugh the entire discussion out of court. There is an ever-increasing number accepting the point of view of Professor Jacks, that the question of immortality forms the background, sometimes unnoticed—often obscured, but always present—to at least three-fourths of the philosophical speculation that has taken place in the world.

Not enough attention has been given to the part it has played as a motive in promoting speculation, and the subject is awaiting treatment by a thinker who is competent to deal with it. Even philosophers who say nothing about it—and it has become a fashion with many to pass it over in silence—owe more to these promptings, both positive and negative, than they seem to be aware of.

In the light of such a statement, it seems appropriate that we consider fairly and frankly the question of Job: "If a man die, shall he live again?" It is not only Job's question—it is a perennial question that must be thought through by every generation.

Thoreau may have satisfied himself when he said: "One world at a time, Parker!" This answer would not have brought comfort to Job, and it will not satisfy the larger number who live in our day and generation. I cannot know myself, until I know whether death is a doorway, or a descent into nothingness. Am I a soul, or am I only a body? Am I to live three score years and ten, or am I to live on through the ages?

Paul's logic was, "If the dead rise not, let us eat and drink, for tomorrow we die." A writer who attempted to enrich this life by denying the next, said: "Now we do not believe in any other life, and we propose to have our share of the good things of the world as they go."

It seems reasonable to believe that we may have our share of the good things of the world without precluding the hope of another life; in fact, it seems more reasonable that we shall share in the good things of this world more equitably if we believe in a world to come. If the experiences of this life had as their purpose the developing and directing of the soul, not only through the gateway of death, but into a richer, fuller, friendlier life after we have "crossed the bar," we should not be so self-seeking in our desires to eat, drink and be merry. Such a view encourages devotion, self-sacrifice and service. These are the good things in this or in the future life.

Some time ago I debated the subject, "Does Death End Life?" with Clarence Darrow, and this was his conclusion: I believe there is not a scrap of evidence anywhere in the universe to prove any such belief. You can buy everything that makes a man at the drug store for about five dollars. His structure is wonderfully like the structure of any other machine.

Mr. Darrow seemed quite as confident of his ability to create man as he felt his ability to prove that man's destiny was death, yet I think we can agree that though he has captured many jurors, he has never created one. Though he believes that man shares the same destiny as all other animals, and that his self-consciousness adds nothing of an eternal quality of life, he has never been able to get an acquittal with any other animal in the jury box.

Without discussing mechanism and teleology, let me suggest that if we agree that Mr. Darrow is right in calling the organism an engine, Professor J. A. Thompson is also right in reminding us that it is a self-stoking, self-repairing, self-preserving, self-adjusting, self-increasing, self-reproducing engine and conscious of the end, the larger life.

The general purpose of this sermon is not to answer Mr. Darrow's objections. Voltaire said that immortality had been discussed for four thousand years in four thousand ways. Such a statement strengthens rather than weakens reasons for such a belief. It testifies to the virility of the subject. So has Mr. Ingersoll testified to the vigor of the belief, when at his brother's grave he spoke: "But in the night of death, hope sees a star, and listening love can hear the rustle of a wing. He who sleeps here, when dying, mistaking the approach of death for the return of health, whispered with his latest breath, 'I am better now.' Let us believe in spite of doubts and dogmas and tears and fears, that these dear words are true of the countless dead."

The general purpose in mentioning the names of these men is not to answer their arguments, for if I had only one sermon to preach on immortality, I would want it to be positive rather than negative. The men are referred to as illustrations of the types of modern minds that do not agree with our affirmations. It is just as wise to guard against dogmatism as it is to guard against skepticism.

When man knew least about this world, he supposedly knew most about the other world. We will certainly be able to remove some of our misunderstandings if we distinguish carefully between a belief and an intellectual statement of that belief. It is not so important for us to defend truth, as to seek honestly to discover and loyally to follow truth.

It will be well for us to keep in our minds the happenings of history. It was Comte, the French philosopher, who said it was no use trying to study the nature of fixed stars; that was something forever beyond the reach of the human intellect. Shortly after his funeral, the spectroscope was discovered, and we know about fixed stars. Some man in England, convinced, and attempting to convince, that a steamship could not cross the Atlantic Ocean, had his belief vanish in the presence of a demonstration. A modern Thomas in America, who had more time than talent, worked diligently to prove that an airship could never fly across the Atlantic. He had a theory, but he overlooked one fact—the fact of Lindbergh.

Let me say now, since I will not have occasion to refer to it later, that we are apt to overlook one of the facts if we fail to consider the work of the Society for Psychical Research. It was Gladstone who said, referring to the work of the Society: "It is the most important work that is being done in the world—by far, the most important." The purpose of the Society is not to commit its members to any theory, but to find out if possible, what is true.

I, personally, have never been able to understand why some ministers assume such an infallible air, or make such a sweeping, dogmatic denial, or show such little interest or sympathy with and in the efforts of men who are trying to ascertain whether or not it is possible to demonstrate the teaching of Jesus in the gospel which these preachers have been preaching since the day of their ordination.

When Mesmer discovered what was later called "mesmerism," his discovery was scoffed at by many of the wise as nonsense. Even a scientific committee, appointed to investigate, made what they thought to be an honest review, and reported the matter as fraud and humbug. What intelligent man in the world today would deny hypnotism?

If you think that any such effort at communication can be nothing more than telepathy between living persons, may I remind you of the statement made by Professor Douglas MacIntosh—"If mind in its relation to body is independent enough to make telepathy under certain conditions a fact, it seems not unreasonable to think that mind may be independent enough to continue to exist and act when set free from the body at death."

If I had only one sermon to preach on Immortality, I should not hope to assume the attitude of a dogmatist; rather I should prefer to remind all those who hear or read, that ignorance scoffs while wisdom seeks the truth; and then we should pray with our minds and our hearts: "Lord, open our eyes, that we may see wondrous things out of thy law."

As we look to our lines of evidence for belief in Immortality, science says it is possible; philosophy says it is probable; religion says it is affirmable. Science says it may be; philosophy says it should be; religion says it must be.

Professor William Wright, in his *Student's Philosophy of Religion*,[1] has an interesting and illuminating discussion on "Immortality as a Known Fact," and he first mentions Biological Immortality as an unquestionable fact. Whatever may be the truth of the various biological theories of heredity in detail, it is a fact that life physically perpetuates itself.

The second known fact that he names is Spiritual or Social Immortality. In this sense, great men never

[1] The Macmillan Company.

die. I call attention to this discussion because it serves as a point of contact between what Professor Wright calls speculative forms of immortality, and immortality as a known fact. It will be the purpose of what follows to lend emphasis to the belief in Personal Immortality. That the Soul, Self, or Personality is to survive the experience that we call death; that it is to emerge, or "pass through it," to be clothed in a spiritual body—a body suitable for and adaptable to the new environment—is the contention of this sermon.

THE SCIENTIFIC POSSIBILITY OF IMMORTALITY

Professor Wright says: "Immortality of some sort, in which the contents of the individual's consciousness is preserved at death, is possible, so far as our present scientific knowledge goes."

In an effort to discover how a distinguished group of scientists, including physicists, biologists, historians, sociologists and psychologists, would express themselves in reference to belief in Personal Immortality, Professor James H. Leuba gathered, by means of a questionnaire, a large number of answers from this distinguished group. The answers showed that about one-half of the number believed in Personal Immortality.

Professor Wright says, and I think rightly so, that it is evident that those who are in doubt whether or not there is Personal Immortality, do not believe that it is scientifically impossible; otherwise they certainly would disbelieve in it. So it is not a misinterpretation of Professor Leuba's statistics to say that at least two-thirds of his scientists regard Personal Immortality as, at any rate, possible.

We can be certain that these figures are not prejudiced in favor of Personal Immortality, for it is a belief in which the author himself strongly disbelieves. One thing was noticed so far as the questionnaire was concerned,—that the number of those who disbelieve in Personal Immortality is greater among the biologists and psychologists, whose fields of investigation bring them into closer contact with questions of the relation between mind and body. The question is, "Does consciousness depend upon the normal functioning of brain cells, and can it survive the destruction of the brain at death?" To assume that it cannot survive is to assert, according to Professor William James, that the function is productive in the sense in which we say that steam is the function of the teakettle; light of the electric circuit; power of the moving waterfall. There are transmissive functions, as in the case of a colored glass, a prism, or a refracting lens, which do not produce the light, but transform its rays in manifold forms. The contention of Professor James is that the mind might be a function of the brain in either one of these senses.

Professor William Hanna Thomson says: "Those reasoners who attempt to explain Personality away by saying that it is only the condition of our make-up at the time being, evidently imagine that we are ourselves, according to the state of the atoms or ions of our brain. This theory is disposed of by the demonstration that our mentality is wholly unilateral in our brain, and is made so by nothing in the brain itself, either before birth, or at birth.

"This as you see, compels the admission that the thinker and his brain are two separate things—the brain like the hand, being only the instrument of the thinker, and to think of Personality which thinks, proposes and wills, as automatic, is a self-contradiction in terms. The Soul as a center and agent of mental activity, can change the form and direction of its activities, but its energies themselves never cease. Its spiritual energy can never be spent and vanish. It is that bit of immortal energy that can never die. The Soul, or Self, the first piece of reality we indubitably know, is constituted as a Personality. We think, we feel, we will;—we do these three things and we never do more or less; therefore we see our Soul or Self as a reality, competent to survive the shock of death, and weave around itself a new body, adapted to its new condition."

Professor McDougal says that all processes alien in quality and behavior to bodily processes, must find the cause of such phenomena in the Soul. The Soul is a being that possesses or is the sum of definite capacities to produce sensations, feelings, meanings, memories, connotations and judgments, in interaction with the body. Such a Soul can survive the body at death.

A most interesting illustration appeared in a scientific journal some time ago, relating how a French

288

scientist, Professor Charles Henry,[1] declared that the human Soul—that mysterious thing that is not a thing, which man has accepted only through faith, can now be measured. "It is the first time," says the writer, "science has ever admitted tangible proof of the Soul's existence. Religion is right. We never completely die. There is a certain electrical radiation or biological vibration that goes on and on. Set free by death, it seeks another envelope or body, because only by so doing, can it establish its equilibrium."

It may be difficult for most of us to grasp the full significance of the dependence or independence between body and mind. It may be equally as difficult for us to conceive of Soul or Spirit. We may be helped to an understanding by hearing these interrogations of Mr. Francis Miller: "Did surgical science ever find a thought in the brain of a human being? Did it ever locate an idea in the mind of man? Did it ever find a railroad engine, a radio instrument, a steel foundry, an automobile, a fifty-story building or a Brooklyn Bridge in the head of man?"

And yet he says we all know that these emanated from and grew out of an idea,—an intangible, undiscovered thought in the mind of man. Everything that exists,—every mechanism, every structure that man has created is but the materialization of one of these unmeasurable thoughts or invisible ideas,—yet no surgeon has ever been able to dissect one,—perform

[1] "Measuring the Human Soul," in *Popular Science Monthly,* December, 1925.

an operation on one, or remove one from the human brain.

What scientist ever saw a thought,—yet who would deny that it is the most powerful thing in the world? Did anyone ever find love or hate in the heart of man, or seated anywhere in his anatomy? Did anyone ever locate courage or fear, joy or sorrow, good or bad, in the organism of man?

To reflect upon some such questions makes it easier, it seems to me, to accept the possibility of continuation of the Soul or Spirit, after the physical body is dissolved.

THE PHILOSOPHICAL PROBABILITY OF IMMORTALITY

The philosopher would say that if man is not immortal, he ought to be.

If man ought to be immortal, we need not shy away from a reasonable faith in such a belief, for reasonable faith is a postulate of scientific inquiry. As we find ourselves in the universe, it is natural that we seek to know more about the universe. If we fail in this connection to consider immortality, we take the light from the ever present, yet ever distant urge that gives courage and strength to life.

"We cannot think," says Professor James H. Snowden, "that the slow, progressive struggle that leads up to its highest form and finally culminates in the personality of man, arrives only to end in nothingness at the top. Such a belief robs the whole process of meaning, and the mathematical conclusion of such a world would be, the sum total of the universe equals nothing. We believe, rather, that the same process that carried it so far, logically requires that it go on to the full realization of all its struggles and hopes and prophecies, in the Life Immortal.

"This conclusion," says Dr. Snowden, "is required by the very rationality of the universe. Man himself, thinks the universe, and thereby rises above it, and puts it under his feet." [1]

As I seek to understand the relationship that should exist between God, the universe and myself, I do not shy away from law; I discover it as a means to my liberty. They are not enemies; they are allies,—just as I discover that mechanism and spirit are allies; and as I discover my plan and purpose, I see this continual expansion, this entering into richer and wider experiences that brings me to a greater appreciation of the quality of life,—life that opens into infinite vistas,— Life Eternal.

It was such a conception that led Mr. Balfour to say: "We know too much about matter to be materialists." It was such a view that led Professor John Scott Haldane to develop the thesis that the material world, which has been taken for a world of blind mechanism, is in reality the spiritual world, seen very partially and imperfectly, and the only real world is the spiritual world. Immortality is a steadying and building force in our world. Its foundation is respect for human nature, and not contempt for it. The social order is

---

[1] *Can We Believe in Immortality?* Fleming H. Revell.

built upon this consummation, and we make stable the social order by a widening vision of the probability of the future of the race.

We are witnessing today in many places, chaotic waste and inhuman brutality, and if we lose sight of the pragmatic implications of immortality, why would not this be true? Any philosophy that throws doubt on the worthwhileness of life is working, whether it is so intended or not, for disorder, discouragement and disintegration.

"The personality of a good man is the most valuable thing we know. If such personalities can survive death and continue to develop and to be of service, the universe is richer in value than if these personalities are bound to perish.

"Personality, as we experimentally know it, is not a powerless, inoperative consequence of manoeuvring atoms. Personality is effectively causative. Without doubt, it has been built up within the scaffolding of the brain, and at least temporarily, depends upon the brain. But it transcends its original condition, it rises above the material forces of the world, it shapes them, controls them, commands even its own psychological processes to such good purpose that from new systems of education to new means of locomotion, mind increasingly masters the world, and the boundaries of its mastery are as yet visible. This fact of personality's emergence and controlling power, its subjection of physical processes to spiritual ideals, its transcendence above the world and lordship over it, is the most amazing and revealing fact in the universe, and any interpretation of the universe which denies to it regulative influence is like an endeavor to interpret the solar system without noticing the sun." [1]

That these spiritual values and experiences are cut down with the body is not a rational, natural or normal inference. These experiences and values are not to perish in the "fatal refrigeration of a congealed planet." Ralph Waldo Emerson answers affirmatively:

> What is excellent
> As God lives, is permanent.

THE RELIGIOUS AFFIRMABILITY OF IMMORTALITY

The religionist has ever clung to some form of belief in life after death. A historian says: "I think there is no exception; no type so ignorant, so degraded, so low, so uncultured, has been found that it did not hold in some form, the belief that there was that in man which death could not touch."

Such beliefs have developed as life has developed, and I have no intention of tracing that history. Paul says: "He hath abolished death and brought life and immortality to light through the gospel."

We may hope for much that we do not find in the teachings of Jesus concerning death and the future life. He does not discuss the origin of death. Some people lay great emphasis upon Jesus' statement to

---

[1] *Spiritual Values and Eternal Life,* by Harry Emerson Fosdick. Harvard University Press.

the penitent thief: "Today thou shalt be with me in paradise." Other than such a statement, we have little from his lips as to the abode of the departed spirits. If we examine the teachings of Jesus concerning the kingdom, he says: "The kingdom of God cometh not by observation. If they say, lo, here, or lo, there, pay no attention to them, for the kingdom of God is within you." It seems that Jesus expected the kingdom of God to be established on this earth of ours—that it is here in true and noble hearts.

"God is spirit; and they that worship him must worship him in spirit and in truth." I am not unfamiliar with the difficulty of obtaining the personal opinion of Jesus without having a letter or even a line from his pen. We must construct his views from portraits by his disciples who held in affectionate memory his sayings and doings. It is almost impossible to conceive of a statement or a restatement of the belief or beliefs of Jesus, that were different from the popular beliefs of his time, without having his sayings colored to some extent by the generally-accepted doctrines of his day.

Jesus takes immortality for granted. Just before the crucifixion, Jesus—according to the portrait of John—is discussing with his disciples the matter of his going away, or the matter of death, or life after death. His destination is to the Father, and his purpose is that they are to be received by him in this prepared place.

THE POSSIBILITY OF PERSONAL IMMORTALITY

Some one has said that if we are to accept the teachings of Jesus as of authority, then those who have been intimately associated here will naturally gravitate together in that spiritual life, and will renew the felicity and the sweetness of their old-time associations.

Jesus said to the disciples: "You know the way to where I am going";—but Thomas said: "Lord, we do not know where you are going,—and how are we to know the way?" And the answer of Jesus is significant, for, as has well been pointed out, he does not say it is above the sky; he does not say it is off on some distant star in space; he does not point in any direction,—east, west, north, or south; he says: "I am the real and living way; I am the Way, the Truth and the Life." Later in the discussion, when Jesus is talking about eternal life, he uses this striking sentence: "And this is eternal life, that they know thee the only real God, and him whom thou hast sent, even Jesus Christ."

Whatever may be our interpretation, it must harmonize with the Christian gospel of the Fatherhood of God, as taught by Christ in the Gospels. This he lived to indicate and died to vindicate. When we speak of these spiritual values and experiences, we are not speaking theories or hypotheses; we are speaking facts.

"Alpha Centauri, is no more of a fact than is Wordsworth, writing the Ode on Immortality. The universe produced both of them. The universe cannot be understood without treating both of them as bases for induction. The cosmos did not stop with newts, but

295

went on to Newton; it did not exhaust itself in crystals but produced Christ. Goodness, truth, beauty, love, —these are existent facts, forcibly effectual in our world, and no explanation of existence that treats them and their personal embodiment as accidental aliens does justice to their factual aspect."

When we speak of life after death, we enter a domain of speculation. We must use certain figures, certain thought forms, and certain inferences, but is not that also true of our physical world today? What are time, space, matter, motion, cause and effect, but instruments that are adopted by the mind for limited purposes? When darkness greets our gaze, is it too much to suppose that light has broken upon the Soul? May not sunset to us mean sunrise to the Soul?

The central purpose of life, as well as the central theme in the teaching of Jesus, points to this belief in Personal Immortality—not that a dead man lives, but that a living man never dies;—"For whosoever liveth and believeth in me shall never die."

Death is like passing from one room to another. There is no standing still or slipping backward. Better absolute annihilation than either of these. It is my very firm conviction that we shall enter the next life very much as we leave this one—that heaven is not to be a place of hosannas and hallelujahs—of golden streets and pearly gates, and we are not to have great orchestras banked in balconies of clouds, but that we will go on in a logical process, developing and unfolding the potentialities of the Soul that have hitherto had no medium for consummation.

Our great control is to be our thoughts. There we will have an opportunity to develop that which can never be developed to a state of perfection here. Do not misunderstand. I am not saying that perfection will be reached immediately upon my passing into the Soul Country. I believe, rather, the opposite: that it will not be reached immediately, but that I shall have shed my shackles and that I will be willing to launch out—not with weights, but wings—not wings that are pictured on angels' shoulders, but wings of thought,—wings of sympathy,—wings of concern,—wings of understanding,— wings of love and mutual consolation; and the purpose of that process will be to develop perfect love, perfect beauty, perfect justice,—three things that I have never grasped the full scope of, in this earthly tabernacle that now provides a dwelling-place for my Soul. That is and is to be God's unfettered instrument of progress.

Afraid of Immortality?

AGNES MAUDE ROYDEN

Agnes Maude Royden, the foremost woman preacher in the English speaking world, represents the women in this series of sermons on Immortality.

Miss Royden first became known when she was the Associate Pastor of City Temple in London during the pastorate of Dr. J. Fort Newton, another of our contributors to this book. Miss Royden was the Associate at City Temple from 1917 to 1920.

Recently she has transferred her leadership to the Guildhouse, Eccleston Square, London, S.W.I. She was born in 1876, received her education at Cheltenham Ladies' College and at Lady Margaret Hall, Oxford. She worked at the Victoria Woman's Settlement for three years at Liverpool.

She was a strong force in the National Woman's Suffrage Society and edited The Common Cause until 1914, writing and speaking on various phases of the woman's movement.

She recently made a tour of the world and when in The United States attracted great attention; large audiences heard her wherever she spoke. Those who heard her came away convinced that they had heard one of the greatest woman preachers living to-day. Deeply spiritual and tender, she won the hearts of her American audiences as few male visitors from England do.

She is the author of several books which have been republished in the United States and which have been widely read in this nation, among which are: *The Hour and The Church, The Friendship of God, Christ Triumphant, Sex and Common-Sense, The Church and Woman, I Believe in God,* etc.

Afraid of Immortality?

By Agnes Maude Royden, Guildhouse, London

"I shall be satisfied, when I awake, with thy likeness."
—PSALMS XVII: 15

To some of us at all times, and to all of us perhaps sometimes, the promise of immortality is not so much a hope as a fear. A friend of mine once said to me—"Why do you preachers never preach to those of us who fear immortality? The mere thought of going on and on for ever is not comforting to everyone: it is even horrifying. It is not that we do not believe in immortality and want to; it is that we more than half believe in it and wish that we did not." Then he added, with a twinkle in his eye, that he was tempted to leave instruction in his will that this epitaph should be put upon his tomb:

Don't bother me now,
Don't bother me never.
I want to be dead
For ever and ever.

Such people are not necessarily melancholy people, nor necessarily materialistic, but they *want* "to be dead for ever and ever." They have had enough. It seemed to him, said my friend, that Rodin had some such idea as this when he created that great statue called "The Thinker." Many of you no doubt have seen it. It is the colossal figure of a man, sitting with head bent and eyes looking out into space; the brow is wrinkled with intense thought, the face tense with concentration. At what is he looking? Of what is he thinking? "I will tell you what I think he is looking at," said my friend: "he is looking down the ages, age after age, world after world, state after state, and still he sees forever advancing down the corridors of time, himself, his own personality, his difficult troublesome discordant self. And he says to himself (as I sometimes say to myself), 'Shall I never escape? must I go on for ever and ever?' "

Why is it that most of us sometimes share this feeling? Deep and instinctive as is our clinging to life, few remain unmoved by the strange appeal of that haunting line of Shakespeare's—

\ After life's fitful fever he sleeps well. \

Why is the phrase so moving? Surely because it describes our life so terribly well. For most of us it is indeed a fitful fever: that is the pain of it. We have our hot and cold fits. We have our moments of inspiration—even the most materialistic of us—and our hours of flatness and gloom. We have our hours when we see God, and our days and weeks when we cannot see Him but yet are haunted by the vision that we saw. Such moments come to us, perhaps, when we meet those we love, when we worship together, or when some prophet speaks to us words of inspiration. We

302

catch fire and have our hot fit. It passes. We go out again into the world where everything seems commonplace and the cold fit comes again. We have been with the friends of our Lord on the Mount of Transfiguration and have said, "It is good for us to be here": but we cannot stay there. We come back down the mountain to the jeering crowd, the futile suffering, and the glory dies out of our hearts—or rather it does not and it will not die out but remains a strange perplexing memory to haunt us; and we wish that it would die, once and for all.

Yet the thought of that glory remains with us and by its light we are forced to mean well and sometimes even to do well; and that is our trouble. If we could be one thing or the other, hot or cold, good or bad, gloriously inspired or completely prosaic. The trouble is that we cannot be any of them for long or altogether. This is the fitful fever that destroys our peace.

Sometimes indeed we see people who seem to live altogether on the heights. Probably we misjudge them and should know, if we knew them better, that they too are sometimes discouraged and unbelieving. Still, they come before us radiant, full of power and assurance; and we envy them. Also we are inclined to envy people of the other type—the people who go on comfortably from day to day, not troubled with the exaltation that comes to us and leaves us so desperate when it departs, nor do they suffer from thoughts beyond the reaches of their souls. Perhaps we misjudge them too: I expect we do. I expect they have their moments when they are just as conscious as we are of something beyond this jog-trot life. But, either way, we are tempted to envy people whose life seems for good or evil to be lived on one level, people who do not suffer from the fitful fever of life.

At such times and to such people even the thought of meeting again those whom they love (since, if we are immortal, so must they be) is not enough to take away the dread of immortality. For such people, I realise, that even their love is a fever, though it is the thing that above all we should most wish to be absolutely calm and assured. Love, no more than life, is altogether pure. It seems sometimes absolutely impossible to distinguish between the selfish and unselfish elements of our love. We know from our own experience that only those whom we love can really hurt us, and we know—also from our own experience—that we do often again and again terribly hurt the people who love us. We would make our love entirely "good." We would have it altogether kind. Again, we cannot; and realising this the sensitive soul begins to dread immortality even for the sake of those it loves. What should we hope? Are we for ever to make of our love a grief? Must we for ever pursue the people to whom we have given our hearts, with our jealousies, our possessiveness, our exclusiveness, our fears that they do not love us as much as we love them, our dread lest they will not love us for ever? Must we, who have so often tormented them here, pursue them into another life with our difficult tormenting

304

claims? There is always a fear somewhere in human love, and the fact that we know that it is not so in perfect love only fills us with terror. Our love, it seems, is very far from perfect, and the thought of this discordant passion not only hurting us but wounding those whom we love "for ever and ever" sometimes makes even the bravest of us afraid of immortality and takes the joy out of our "sure and certain hope."

What is that sure and certain hope? Not—for me at least—the mere hope of some kind of survival, but the conviction that discord must die. Discord is created in ourselves by the very fact that we cannot rest content with evil, and from this discord we rightly and deeply desire to escape. It is not, however, from love that we wish to be free but from the fitful fever that touches and shadows *even* our love. We would be delivered from the dreadful self-contempt which comes when we realise that the glorious sense of exaltation, the vision of God, the fulness of love, the inspiration which carried us off our feet for a moment, has left us apparently as limited and narrow, as sordid, selfish and unkind as we were before. It is the promise that our Easter also comes—that "when we wake up after Christ's likeness we shall be satisfied with it"—that makes immortality to be desired.

"We shall be satisfied with it." *Satisfied.* It is a word of heavenly promise. To those who believe it and expect it, immortality is no longer full of dread. We shall be—*satisfied.* That is to say, the discord dies at last. Of course—I see that it must. The very fact that it is such a pain to me to be so discordant convinces me that I must go on until this discord ceases. For I see that in my human experience it is the things that are shoddy and mean that do perish, and the things that are good and well done endure. It is a commonplace of our everyday speech that is, what is good lasts. A well-built house, a well-made piece of furniture, even a well-cut garment—these are the things that last. The one absolutely certain quality that is found in all bad work is simply that it does not last. "That is not good work—it will not last." So we say, not thinking what profound wisdom we utter. "That house—that table—that suit—will last for ever. It is good work." This also we say and do not know that what we are really saying is the same as the poet's thought—"A thing of beauty is a joy for ever."

> A thing of beauty is a joy for ever;
> Its loveliness increases; it will never
> Pass into nothingness . . .

And again

> Only the actions of the just
> Smell sweet and blossom in the dust.

And again, speaking of evil—

> It is the note of evil, for good lasts.

We have not much experience of life, it is true, we human beings. Ours is a very short life and we live on a very tiny planet: but yet it is all that we have with which to guess or reason. And at least it is more reasonable to guess from what, in our small experience, has at least proved universally true, than to suggest a more tragic guess, based on no reason or experience at all. All the experience we have goes to show that it is the evil that passes, the shoddy that wears out, the badly made that crumbles. So it seems at last that discord also must be resolved, since evil cannot last.

> In the still ear the music lies unheard.
> In the rough marble, beauty hides unseen
> To wake the music, and the beauty needs
> The master's touch, the sculptor's chisel keen.
>
> Great Master, touch us with thy skilful hand.
> Let not the music that is in us die.
> Great Sculptor, hew and polish us nor let,
> Hidden and lost, that form within us die.
>
> Spare not the stroke. Do with us as Thou wilt.
> Let there be naught unfinished, broken, marred.
> Complete Thy purpose that we may become
> Thy perfect image, Oh, our God and Lord.

"Let not the music that is in us die." I suppose, for the sake of logical completeness, we must admit that it may die. If all our nature were a discord, we might find peace only by the door of annihilation. If there were nothing good left in us, we must die. But indeed this is a contradiction in terms. As long as there *is* discord it is proof that there is still something of good to survive. I therefore will endure the discord and the otherwise intolerable strain of desiring so much better than I do and dreaming so much more gloriously than I live, for the sake of that ineffable peace which shall come when we resolve our discord, not by the door of annihilation, but because that which is good in us is eternal and that which is evil cannot be so.

So, some day, the vision of God that I have seen so fleetingly, remembered so fretfully, so often actually wished I might forget, will be all that I see. The thought makes me gasp. So satisfying it is, so full of joy, that though I desired to forget it I could not, and the thought of it tormented me. If now I should have it altogether and so be tormented no more? Would not the dread of immortality leave me and the joy of it remain?

Probably to many of us the recollection of some moment of pure love for a human being would be, if we were altogether honest, recognised as the greatest moment in our life. A time when for an hour, a day, a week—longer perhaps—we were able to love without jealousy, without greed, without fear, because we were without greed—with indeed nothing but a rapture of reverence in our hearts. This was indeed a time of perfect joy. If we could go to our beloved and give them and find in them such a joy as that for ever, would immortality be worth while?

To me such things seem after all worth enduring much hardness for. It makes the fitful fever of life more than tolerable—radiant even. Indeed, knowing that there may not be a great deal left of me if, at this moment, all that was dishonest, shoddy and mean, were taken away, I even desire to have longer struggle in this world or another, that there may be more of me for my friends to love and be loved by in the end of time. So let me go on and on, even if I meet myself again and again in those corridors of time, for the end crowns all. "It is the note of evil, for good lasts." That is true, even if it isn't in the Bible! And all that we know of Christ convinces us that this is the "glorious hope of immortality" that he gave us. This is the meaning of that great phrase—"As in Adam all die, even so in Christ shall all be made alive." As all that is fallen, all that is evil, all that is mean and shoddy must die, from the very nature of things, for death is in it, so in Christ shall all be made alive. Nothing that is pure, nothing that is lovely, nothing that is good can die—that also is in the nature of things. After life's fitful fever we shall sleep well and when we wake up after Christ's likeness we shall be satisfied with it.

Do You Dare to Live the Life Immortal?

HENRY HALLAM SAUNDERSON

The Unitarian Church is represented in this volume by Henry Hallam Saunderson. He is a graduate of Harvard University, having received both his M.A. and his D.D. degree from that institution. Dr. Saunderson was ordained as a minister in 1898 and is now the incumbent of the First Parish of Brighton, Mass. He is editor of the *Wayside Pulpit,* which carries his words to literally millions of people every week.

Dr. Saunderson is also an author of distinction. His recent book, *Charles W. Eliot: Puritan Liberal,* was widely discussed and reviewed in the press, with the universal comment that this was a biographical study of first importance. Steeped in the New England tradition, he interprets religion as a glorious heritage and spiritual adventure. His sermon finds a welcome place in this volume.

Do You Dare to Live the Life Immortal?

By HENRY HALLAM SAUNDERSON

"If ye then be risen with Christ, seek those things which are above."
—COL. III: I

WHILE men are in the midst of their active life, they are reminded that it must come to an end, and they ask what the far future has to offer. When volume one of the story of life is finished, will there be any second volume in which it is continued? In thinking of immortality, we are too much inclined to put the first emphasis on length instead of on quality. We seek the assurance that life will be projected on a line that runs into the far future instead of seeking now the higher levels of life, where the assurance of immortality will come unsought. The immortal life has begun, and the eternal world is all about us, waiting to be discovered. Men ask very wistfully if there be another life at the far end of this life; and then Life turns to the questioner and asks him if he dares to live now the life immortal, and offers him the priceless reality as a present attainment.

There is a high bluff on the eastern part of the New England coast from which, on a clear day, may be seen a little speck on the horizon—a tiny rocky island.

Sometimes fishermen, in little boats, venture out to it, and, if the sea is exceptionally smooth, they may make a landing from a little bay of the rocky island. Yet on its rough shores there is always the noise of surf, for the sea is never perfectly calm. The ice and storms of uncounted centuries have polished the rocks. The soil is scanty and almost sterile; and therefore the vegetation is sparse. It offers only harsh conditions for any kind of life.

Yet here the sea-gulls nest in great numbers, and the young gulls begin life under circumstances of great austerity. The restless sea, the flowing tides, the ever-moving winds, and the flying clouds suggest little of sympathy for these little downy creatures. But watch one of them when he has broken his shell. He surveys his harsh surroundings; and soon he stands up and moves about a little. Within an hour he leaves the nest, which is a shallow depression in the rock, and walks directly to the salt water. Without hesitation he trusts himself to the tumbling waves and the flowing tides and the unceasing winds.

He begins the experience of the life for which he is adapted and he fears not the immensities of sea and sky. His first breath is the wind across this desolate island; the first light that comes to his eyes is from this wind-swept sky; and, without instruction or guidance, he turns to the salt sea in the first hour after breaking his shell. An instinct, which is beyond our knowledge or understanding, directs him to his life in the great deep. That instinct does not betray him; and, because he trusts himself to the great deep, it sustains him. He has no fear of life's austerities nor doubt of its sustaining power. If he could put into words what his action implies, he would say to the sea,—"Thou hast made us for thyself, and our hearts are restless until they rest in thee."

It was thus that St. Augustine spoke of human beings surrounded by the infinite and eternal realities of God's presence. We have our little rocky island, the world of our physical senses. But the immortal life is written in our very souls. Around this island are the tides of the Spirit, the winds of the Eternal, the overarching sky of the Infinite. Until we trust ourselves to these measureless realities we do not understand life, nor our own being, nor the spiritual motives that stir within us. We may hesitate to act upon the impulses which impel us toward our normal life in God; but those impulses make us restless. We may seek to disregard them, or to thwart them, and we may misinterpret them; but they never wholly cease. In very simple language, a profound truth was uttered by Phillips Brooks: "We are haunted by an ideal life. It is in our blood and never will be still." Age after age, the great spiritual leaders of the race have reminded men of this truth.

This little rocky island of our material world does not offer an understanding of our own being, nor of our life. We may be very diligent in acquiring possessions, and still go through life unsatisfied. The material world does not account for the powers we possess: the powers of body and mind and spirit. It cannot account for our aspirations nor our highest impulses. It cannot explain even those simple relationships of daily life, our friendships and our affections, —those relationships which make our home and our neighborhoods. In the midst of the commonplaces of daily life we become aware that we have standards of moral value which transcend the commonplace. Why should a man sometimes "lay down his life for his friend"? Why does a mother sometimes "starve for her brood"? Whence does any being, standing empty-handed in the presence of eternal truth, gain the sense of moral values which enables him to say: "To this end was I born, and for this cause came I into the world, that I should bear witness to the truth"? Here are eternal values in the midst of our temporal life. Here are immortal impulses in the midst of the things which "perish with the using." Continually we are being startled by the Infinite; and every moment of such insight teaches us that the world we are living in is not essentially a physical world, and that this higher life is not temporal but eternal.

We seek to know our world; but knowledge will not be complete when we have completed an exact survey of our little rocky island and have followed, to their ultimate conclusions, our lines of logic concerning it. Only a limited part of the world we live in consents to register itself on our physical sense-organs. Only a minor area of it is included in the pattern made by the lines of our reason. "The things which are seen are temporal; but the things which are not seen are eternal." To know our world we must test the eternal and unseen realities; and this test is made by our living. If we wait for knowledge before making the great adventure of living the life immortal, we shall miss that adventure. If we think it is to be deferred until we come to another world, we shall fail to understand this present world. Immortality stands before us with its supreme challenge, saying, "If ye then *be risen* with Christ, seek those things which *are above.*" It asks us this poignant question—"Do you dare to live here and now the life immortal? Are you ready for the adventure of trusting yourself to the tides of the Spirit? Will you live for the sake of the things which cannot perish?"

In the search for the assurance of immortality, men have often sought afar that which can be discovered near at hand. They seek evidence of another world which shall take the place of this world, and of an endless life to open at the far end of the earthly life. They repeat, through the long generations, the ancient question, "If a man die, shall he live again?" Thus they assume the reality of death, and postpone immortality to a shadowy future. So much of the argument for immortality bears a ponderous load of material ideas! It puts emphasis on physical death, and all its attendant circumstances. It calls attention to decay and dissolution and destruction, as they seem to be exemplified in what happens to every physical body of man or animal; and then endeavors to recover a faith

317

in life instead of death. How great the unnecessary burden under which this supreme faith is called upon to travel!

We gaze too long at the tombs of the world. We ask them to swing open their doors and release that which they never could hold as prisoner. We petition the dust of the earth to restore that which never became dust. We request the graves to upheave and give back that which never entered into the grave. We ask Death to reveal to us the mystery of Life and then we wonder why the answer is not given. We declare that we are seeking the proof of immortality even while we give undue emphasis to all that is associated with mortality. Why address the grave when what we want is the answer of Heaven?

How much there is, of human belief, which uses, as its foundation, the assumption that our immortal spirits are dependent on our mortal bodies! Paul pointed out the folly of that assumption, and reversed the emphasis. The spirit builds the body, and it shall build anew according to its needs. When a sower goes forth to sow his grain, he does not expect to recover from the ground the seed he has scattered. Rather does he go forth in the time of harvest to gather that which the miracle of life has created anew. He forgets the seed which was dissolved in the ground and rejoices in the grain which has grown in the light of Heaven.

In tracing the Christian hope of immortality to its source, men have made the most minute study of the tomb near Calvary, and of every recorded word concerning the physical body of Christ. Not enough emphasis has been placed on the beautiful truth that the tomb was in the midst of a garden and that the immortal spirit of Christ was discovered in the midst of the flowers, in the dawn of a day of early spring. We are inclined to forget that the tomb was opened not from within but from without; that the stone was rolled back not by the hands which had been the hands of the Carpenter of Nazareth, but by hands that had never known mortality. The Spirit of Christ never died, never was shut within the tomb, never had its place behind the great stone, and never was imprisoned by the seal that was placed upon that stone. Christ lived the immortal life even while he went about among men; he lived while his body was taken from the cross; he lived while his friends, in sorrow, on that strange Sabbath Day, prepared spices which they afterwards threw away in their joy; he came in the gray of dawn to that garden to meet those who loved him best and to reveal himself to them; but his spirit had not died. Let us not try to imagine his immortal spirit, through the night before the first Easter, sitting in the tomb waiting for release; but rather let our minds hold the picture of his spirit coming, with the first rays of morning light, into that garden where immortality was brought to light.

How strange it is that, in the study of the record of the days that followed, men have sought the material things rather than the spiritual; and have endeavored to find proof of immortality in the temporal rather than the eternal! Doubting Thomas stands not merely as an individual, slow of heart, but as the representative of a multitude who demand physical evidence of spiritual reality. Great are the words of approval which Christ spoke concerning a different working of many human minds, "Blessed are they that have not seen, and yet have believed."

The greatest proof of the immortality of the Spirit of Christ is the power with which it operated in the time that followed that first Easter. Years after, the Apostle John, who traveled far and wide among the disciples of the risen Christ, observed the moral and spiritual power which was associated with the central faith of these people, the faith in immortality. He said, "Every man that hath this hope in him *purifieth* himself." Human lives were lifted to new levels. Conscious that they were already living the immortal life, these men sought "those things which are above." Moral uplift and spiritual power were the consequences of that greatest faith that the human mind can hold, the faith that life may attain immortal quality and thereby be assured of endless duration.

Such a survey as was made by the Apostle John included journeys in the countries around the eastern end of the Mediterranean Sea, where there was a comparatively compact community of Christian churches. Yet a survey of the Christian world today would show that

320

millions of men derive, from their faith in immortality, that same incentive to live the higher life. And when inquirers come, asking in all sincerity for the proof of immortality, it is not the *logic* but the *dynamic* of it that most surely carries conviction. When the messengers of Christ go out to win men to this faith they may go equipped with argument; but better is it to carry to men the challenge, "Do you dare to live, here and now, the life that deserves to last forever?" Strange it is how the fear of death vanishes when men assert greatly the power of life! When life is lifted to the higher moral and spiritual levels, the conviction of immortality is not difficult to attain.

This is, indeed, an ancient discovery, but it is also very modern. It means finding God as a living Presence. It means making the will of God the guide and inspiration of daily living. It means entering into a close and vital comradeship with Him. Such a discovery is always new for it never can grow old. But it means that life is illuminated with a sudden glory and the world is lighted with a glowing radiance. To the newly opened eyes of the spirit, the unseen world becomes visible. The inaudible voice of the Eternal is heard to speak clearly. This is not an abstract discovery, nor is it reached at the end of a logical process; but it comes as the necessary consequence of living the higher life. To live for the immortal realities means that we are already immortal. To trust the tides of the Spirit means that we learn that we are sustained by them. To consecrate life to the doing of the will of God means that we discover the meaning of life and the significance of our own personality. This new meaning in life comes with the greatest moral challenge and the finest spiritual incentive.

This discovery of the Divine Presence does not come by searching afar. "The word is very nigh unto thee, in thy mouth, and in thy heart, that thou mayest do it." Yet because God is so vast, men have sometimes thought that He could be found only afar; just as they think of the immortal life as hidden in another world. Age after age there have been great spiritual leaders who have endeavored to impress upon the minds of the people, of their own generation, this truth of the nearness of God and the immediacy of our discovery of Him. To the seeker who imagines that the desired goal is at the far end of a long journey, St. Augustine says, "Thither one journeyeth not in ships, nor in chariots, nor on foot; for to journey thither, nay, even to arrive there, is nothing else but to will to go."

It was of this discovery, just at hand and not remote, that Whittier wrote,

> I break my pilgrim staff. I lay
>   Aside the toiling oar;
> The angel sought so far away
>   I welcome at my door.
>
> And all the jarring notes of life
>   Seem blending in a psalm;
> And all the angles of its strife
>   Slow rounding into calm.

DO YOU DARE TO LIVE THE LIFE IMMORTAL?

And so the shadows fall apart,
And so the west winds play;
And all the windows of my heart
I open to the day.

Sometimes the poet discovers what the theologian misses; and the mystic beholds, by direct vision, what the logician fails to find by his laborious processes. To the weary traveler, who has missed the object of his search just because he has traveled so laboriously, the Divine Voice speaks, saying,—"Be still, and know that I am God."

The deepest intuitions of the soul shall not betray us but rather bring us to the great discovery. Convictions, too deep for logical proof, assure us that goodness is eternal; that truth is immortal; that integrity is deathless; that love is everlasting. To live for these things guides us toward the discovery of God and the assurance of life everlasting.

Christocentric Keys

FREDERICK FRANKLIN SHANNON, D.D., LL.D.

Frederick Franklin Shannon was born in Morris County, Kansas, in the heart of the wheat country, February 11th, 1877, and had his schooling in Webb College, Tennessee, and Harvard.

He was ordained as a Methodist minister in 1899 and served his first churches in the mountain state of West Virginia. From his first little church in Logan, West Virginia he was suddenly called to Grace Church, Brooklyn, N. Y., where he served from 1904 to 1912 and from there went to The Reformed Church on The Heights where he was pastor from 1912 to 1919. Since 1920 he has been pastor of Central Congregational Church in Chicago, an eloquent successor to Dr. Gunsalus, famous preacher of another generation.

Dr. Shannon has always been one of America's most eloquent preachers and Chautauqua lecturers as was his predecessor in Central Church, Chicago, but since the days of the Radio Broadcast he has become one of the four or five most popular Radio Preachers, from his centrally located pulpit in Chicago.

He is the author of a round dozen volumes of unusual sermons which have a wide circulation among preachers themselves. Of poetic temperament one of the powers of his preaching is the sense of music, such as Bishop William A. Quayle used to have.

Some of his more popular books are: *The Unfathomable Christ, The Infinite Artist, The New Greatness.* His address is 6927 Oglesby Avenue, Chicago, Ill.

Christocentric Keys

By FREDERICK FRANKLIN SHANNON, MINISTER OF CENTRAL
CHURCH, CHICAGO, ILL.

"When I saw him, I fell at his feet like a dead man; but he laid his
hand on me, saying, Do not be afraid; I am the First and Last, I
was dead and here I am alive for evermore, holding the keys that
unlock death and Hades."

—REV. 1: 17, 18

As I understand it, the Christian religion contains
within its being a twofold reaction—the reaction
of man's soul to God and the reaction of God to man's
soul. Within this human and divine reaction is the
continuous action of the universe—that is, somewhere
within and between the Soul of God and the Soul of
Man the vast and immeasurable cosmos is at uninter-
rupted play, moving ever on toward a goal preordained
by Intelligence and Love.

Now, man's reaction to God is not invariably that
of peace, joy, and creative calm. Sometimes, as in
the text, the reaction is fear, terror, panic, paralysis.
"When I saw him, I fell at his feet like a dead man."
Such words may be regarded in some quarters as
merely a symptom of disease; nevertheless, they are
more in league with the loftiest expressions of
Christian character and conduct than they are with

the emaciated and ineffectual editions thereof, amounting, as they frequently do, to something dangerously akin to paradise. Then, also, here is God's reaction to man. "But he laid his hand on me, saying, Do not be afraid." What! Is it possible for one to be filled with terror one moment and then to be lifted by tenderness the next? Does not something like this glow through the very heart of Christian history even while it throbs through the soul of our own troubled day?

My subject is, "Christocentric Keys." I wish to use the text, out of which the subject comes, not so much from the standpoint of exposition as of furnishing an opportunity of expressing my faith and reason in and for the life immortal.

I

CONSIDER THE CHRISTOCENTRIC KEY TO COSMIC ORIGINS AND ENDINGS

"I am the First and the Last." The human mind has always been haunted in a twofold direction. First, as to the beginnings of things. How did the universe come by its initial urge? What was behind the beginning? We see a million effects; what is their cause? Do things make themselves, and then keep themselves going forever and ever? These are some of the questions the mind inevitably asks with reference to cosmic origins, whether in the form of electrons or stars, animals or angels, mud or men.

A second phase of the same problem is: How and when shall the earth, the solar system, indeed the immeasurable universe of matter, or of universes within universes, come to an end? Or is there to be an end at all? Is science justified in its conclusion that the material framework of things must either be destroyed or transformed? If so, must the change be wrought by fire or cold? Ultimately, shall it all be burned up or frozen up? Whatever the answer may be, the human mind, whether wearing philosophic, scientific, or religious dress, is continuously walking in the midst of these problems and asking them questions. There are indeed many shut doors within the bewildering universe to which we belong.

Yet, just because a door is shut, does not render the situation hopeless. The very fact that there is a door imparts hope and courage. For a door leads to something; otherwise, there would be no need of it. When we consider, moreover, that a door at least suggests a key that may unlock it is there not a definite increase of hope and courage? Now I believe that God in Christ—the most adequate philosophic and religious formula that has so far made its home in the mind of man—furnishes a competent key, one by which all shut doors must be finally opened.

"I am the First and the Last." Here is the key named *Infinite Personality*. It is as good as any key that has come within the grasp of man; and a great multitude of the most brilliant minds, as well as the noblest characters, hold that it is much better than any other. I doubt if we shall ever be able to explain, absolutely, the subtle and intricate relations which the

Eternal Mind sustains to the universe of matter and energy. Yet this fact need not smite us with the paralysis of agnosticism. Rather, it seems to me, should we rejoice in our faith in a God at once so great as to include the universe as the sea includes the waves and so intimate as the body indwelt by the mind that knows itself. I am not interested particularly, just at the moment, what theologic or philosophic cast the thought takes, whether monism, pantheism, or theism. What I am interested in is the fact of the grandeur and goodness of the Godhead unveiled in Christ; and that fact unquestionably is that cosmic origins and endings are within the keeping of a Self-conscious Personality, unutterably good and eternally purposeful. This is just the theistic idea that Mind is before Matter unless, indeed, we think that Matter is fundamentally superior to Mind.

I say that the supreme minds of the world, notwithstanding the variations in their expression of it, believe and teach the priority of the Divine Mind. "It sounds at first singular," says Kant, "but it is none the less certain, that the understanding does not derive its laws from nature, but prescribes them to nature." "The material world is realized idea," says Bowne, to whom philosophy, to be its best, has yet to grow up. Essentially, there is nothing in nature which accounts for the origin of Mind, whether in God or man; and I say this in full view of the long and subtle processes through which, on the manward side, brain becomes the instrument of Mind. Thus, in keeping with the high-mindedness of the centuries, the modern thinker insists that "the chemico-physical explanation of the universe goes but a little way. These are the tools of the creative process, but they are not the process nor its prime cause. Start the flame of life going, and the rest may be explained in terms of chemistry; start the human body developing, and physiological processes explain its growth; but why it becomes a man and not a monkey—what explains that?" In all its intellectual search and experiential reaction, man has found but one competent answer, and it falls within the category of Infinite Personality—even the living God and Father of our Lord and Saviour Jesus Christ. Within all beginnings and all endings, whether of vast island universes or ultra-microscopic electronic systems of wonderful orderliness, religion alone holds the key that can open the immeasurable doors waiting to be unlocked. With infinite insight and incomparable majesty, it says, "I am the First and the Last."

This, then, is the ground of my belief in human immortality. That which is behind and within the universe is Superconscious Intelligence, the Spirit of Infinite Goodwill infinitely aware of Himself, the very God who so loves the world of humanity that He gave and gives His only begotten Son, that whosoever believes in him, shall not perish, but have eternal life. God is a spirit, man is a spirit, and the destiny of these two is inseparably bound up with each other. This is either a fact or it is not a fact. Believing it to be the most transcendent qualitative fact the human mind can think, I heartily believe not merely in the deathlessness of every individual human, but in the mental growth and spiritual increase of every human individual through all eternity. Therefore, neither infinite time nor infinite matter nor infinite energy can touch, in the smallest degree, that which does not belong in their categories. The human soul is the offspring of the living God, who is not the God of the dead, because He cannot possibly be, without contradicting His own beginningless being, unto whom all humans live and in whom all humans have their immortal self-realization.

> What care I though falls the sky
>   And the shivering earth to a cinder turn?
> No fires of doom can ever consume
>   What never was made nor meant to burn!

> Let go the breath! There is no death
>   To a living soul, nor loss, nor harm,
> Not of the clod is the life of God—
>   Let it mount, as it will, from form to form.

II

THINK, ALSO, OF THE CHRISTOCENTRIC KEY TO THE DOOR OF DEATH

"I was dead." Men speak of death as The Great Mystery. In this they do well; only the foolish and inconsiderate speak otherwise. Not only mysterious, death is unimaginably familiar, being one of the unfathomable processes whereby life earns its own living. Look anywhere within the plant world. Every root, every flower, every blade of grass, every stalk of corn says, "I was dead." Look at the animal world. Every bird, every bee, every fish, every deer says, "I was dead." In short, throughout the whole natural world, death is the servant of life. All plants and animals owe their being to the process called death. If Infinite Personality is alone commensurate with the concept of cosmic origins and endings, do we not require, also, a very much larger, if not an infinite category, for the meaning of death? Certainly, our ordinary meanings are pitiably small. For, as commonly understood, there is no such fact as death in the natural world. That which appears to be dead, static, inert, is, on closer view, profoundly, deathlessly alive. If this is true, there is little wonder that, in accounting for mind as embodied in humanity, the philosopher concludes that man is "not a planetary or transitory being; he persists as very man among the cosmic and eternal things."

I believe that Christ holds, absolutely, the key to the door of death. He unlocks, for mortals, the awful door before which the ages instinctively stand in awe. How? In the first place, Christ grapples with and solves the terrible problem of sin. And let me add, at once, that our Lord does not deal with sin as a metaphysical theory, a legend out of the past; he faces it as every human being must face it—as essentially an act of mischoice made by every responsible human will. Sin, in this view, allows no one to trace his sinfulness back to some historic or legendary ancestor. I myself am the person I have to reckon with in dealing with the horrible fact of sin; neither fallen angels nor fallen ancestors can bear the responsibility which is my very own and not another's; otherwise, it could not be, either in moral justice or philosophic understanding, my sin.

Yet, in creating my own cup of sin, in mixing the deadly draught it contains, I partake of the deadliest death within the whole universe—the death superinduced by sin. This, I have not the slightest doubt, is the fuller implication of the apostle's words that "the sting of death is sin," as well as the formidable significance of the seer's figure concerning "the second death."

Nobody but Christ comes to triumphant grips with the dreadful fact of sin in human life. He tastes death for every man; he alone knows the bitterness, the deadliness at the roots of the will which, by its own responsible mischoices, creates the appalling fact of spiritual death. Only Christ Jesus—Eternity on the planes of time, Deity within the mysterious meshes of the human—he, and he alone, concocts and administers the antidote for sin. Stopping alongside a California highway, I went a short distance unto the field of a sheep ranch. The suggestion had been made that I might see some rattlesnakes—though, I confess, I was not unduly eager to find them. Soon a shepherd happened along. "Do you ever see any rattlers around here?" I asked. "Yes, indeed," he answered, "only

334

last week a student from the University of California caught five just beyond where you are standing." "Caught them for what?" I asked, moving back toward the roadway. "Oh, to make an antidote, a serum not only for snakebite, but for other maladies." Well, God in Christ brings His own serum, His own antidote for the poison of sin. Tasting death for every man, he dashes the deadliness of the sin-death from the cup of mortality and restores the victim unto the kind and quality of immortal vigor which ejects spiritual death from the house of life.

In the second place, Christ verifies the fact of human deathlessness. No people have doubted human survival. Individuals have had such doubt and still have it; but mankind as a whole, in its most backward as well as in its most enlightened branches, always instinctively and intuitively affirms the immortality of the soul. Christ verifies this intuition, demonstrates the reality of the age-old dream, proves the fact that haunted Plato's mind and troubled Kant's categories. He says, "I *was* dead; I experienced death, the seeming past tense of life, that I might prove the present tense of spiritual reality, the life which is life indeed. I hold the key that unlocks the door of speculation; at my behest it opens wide upon the homelands of the life that becomes more abundant as the ages multiply."

Verily, the Lord Christ brings life and immortality to light! "Immortality," says Channing, "is the glorious discovery of Christianity. Before Christ immortality was a conjecture or a vague hope. Jesus, by

335

His teaching and resurrection, has made it a certainty." In other words, God, in the soul of humanity, gives the theorem of immortality, while God in Christ proves that theorem in the field of history, adding indisputable evidence of it in every individual indwelt by the Holy Spirit, without whom there may be much speculation and little satisfaction. Only the Spirit of God can clarify the purpose of God for spirits created in the image of God; all other means are inadequate, even as the inadequacy of love is apparent to everyone but lovers, who bear the divine self-evidence of love within their soul of souls. "This is the will of my Father," says the Lover of Eternity, "that everyone that beholdest the Son, and believeth in Him, should have eternal life." And the best treatment that death can expect from Eternal Life is a kind of past tense accommodation which says, after Eternal Life has made its own august uses of death, "I *was* dead."

III

CONSIDER, FINALLY, THE CHRISTOCENTRIC KEY TO THE DOOR OF LIFE

"And here I am alive forever more, holding the keys that unlock death and Hades." Now, if cosmic beginnings and endings are unfathomable, if death is a profound mystery, a fact bigger and profounder than either is Life itself. Tremendously big words are these: Energy, Matter, Unity, Law. Yet, after all, is not Life a bigger, better, and more inclusive term than any or all of the others? If, as our age insists, it is really a living universe with which we have to do, no other conclusion is possible. And standing before the door of life with the Christocentric key in our hand, we have a twofold assurance.

The first is this: Life always has its own way. There may be indirection, circumlocution, countless windings in and out, but never fear! Life always wins. Nothing, it would seem, can ultimately keep life from realizing its own ends. Mortals may never fully know what those ends are; nevertheless, we seem to know enough of the behavior of Life to assert that Life gets its own way in and through the cosmos. Temporarily balked and baffled, Life may be; but permanently beaten, Life never is, nor can be. It somehow stems the tide of matter at every turn, through all its lengths and breadths and depths and heights. I saw a trolley car come to a standstill in the middle of a cross-street in one of our cities. Traffic was quickly blocked; trolley cars, automobiles, and human beings were all caught within the congestion. But only for a time; the human beings did not stand there paralyzed as if nothing could be done about it. As an immediate expedient, some fifty men got around the car and pushed it a short distance. Then another trolley was soon placed behind the dead car and the human power, necessarily inadequate, was no longer required. But the blocked thoroughfare was relieved; the flow of traffic went on again as if nothing had happened. Confessing that it is a crassly mechanical picture for suggesting the livingness, the vitality within the universe, it may serve to hint the fact that there seems to be, in view of what we know of the Creation, no reason for assuming that Life can be definitely blocked or stopped, because there is Something within Life that knows what it wants and knows how to get it. So much for the Big Fact of Life—bigger than Matter, Energy, Law, Unity, or anything else—within the cosmic order.

But in the higher realm of religion there is an equal assurance for the Soul. Important as cosmic order unquestionably is; alluring as the study of stars and electrons must ever be, the Soul is not asked to live and move and have its being in them—and for the very excellent reason that it cannot; it belongs in other and larger ranges of reality. Souls live *on*, *in*, and *by* the living God who, in Christ Jesus, was "dead" as mortals say, not knowing what they mean—and is alive forever more, holding the keys that unlock death and Hades.

Surely, one form of modern inadequacy, bandied about not only by certain philosophies but by articulate religious cults as well, is a kind of fanatical emphasis it places upon the impersonal. And it is all the more inadequate because, in supreme values, personal relations are the soul of the individual and of society. Life, at its best, says that I have the right to judge the universe and history in the light of the highest I know. No matter how far down in the scale of being the highest began to be, it is not the beginning but the ending

338

that is important. "An idea is what it is on its own account here and now," says Bishop McConnell, in his philosophic post-mortem over Professor Barnes. "If we discover it to be false, it is interesting to see how it arose; and if we find it to be true, its origin is also interesting, but the origin does not tell us whether it is itself true or false."

Now the highest truth I know is God in Christ; no matter how it began or where, I think it is true "on its own account." For here is life transcendent, eternal, beyond all the forms of doom and death manifested in lower realms of being. The uplifted Christ lifts humanity to these high summits where God continually makes "Himself an awful rose of dawn." The fact that vast areas of individual, social, political, national, and international life are blind to the reality of God in Christ does not argue that they shall be permanently so. Gravity did not begin to operate with Newton's discovery. Stars not only were, but kept their orbits for a considerable time before Herschel was born. There must have been music in the universe before even the great Beethoven. So the fact that human beings do not practice the ethical and spiritual laws of God in Christ does not invalidate those laws; the time is coming when they shall be as self-evident as the laws of physics and astronomy. For He is the Lord of Life in every realm. Little by little, and with patience divine, God is moving in upon all godless circles to interpret them to themselves and to disclose the ends for which they exist. And those ends, at once near and far away, are revealed in words and meanings so vast, so rich, so various that ages upon ages shall not impoverish their inexhaustible content: "And this is life eternal, that they should know thee the only true God, and him whom thou didst send, even Jesus Christ." In the light of such truth, uttered by the truth Himself, it is well to let Tennyson ask and answer our own question:

Will my tiny spark of being wholly vanish in your deep
    and heights?
Must my day be dark by reason, O ye Heavens, of your bound-
    less nights,
Rush of suns, and roll of systems, and your fiery clash of
    meteorites?

Spirit, nearing yon dark portal at the limit of thy human
    state,
Fear not thou the hidden purpose of that Power which alone
    is great,
Nor the myriad world, His shadow, nor the silent Opener
    of the Gate!